FATHER OF COMFORT

By the same author:
BEHOLD HIS LOVE
HIDDEN IN HIS HANDS
I FOUND THE KEY TO THE HEART OF GOD
MATTER OF LIFE AND DEATH
MIRROR OF CONSCIENCE
MY ALL FOR HIM
PRAYING OUR WAY THROUGH LIFE
REALITIES OF FAITH
REPENTANCE—THE JOY-FILLED LIFE
RULED BY THE SPIRIT
THOSE WHO LOVE HIM
YOU WILL NEVER BE THE SAME

FATHER
OF COMFORT
Daily Readings

Basilea Schlink

Bethany Fellowship, Inc.
Minneapolis, Minnesota

Published by
BETHANY FELLOWSHIP, INC.
6820 Auto Club Road
Minneapolis, Minnesota 55438

German Edition 1965

*Original title: Der Niemand Traurig
Sehen Kann*

*First Published in English 1971
by OLIPHANTS, London*

*Unless otherwise stated all Bible quota-
tions are taken from the Revised
Standard Version of the Bible, copy-
righted 1946 and 1952 by the Division
of Christian Education of the National
Council of the Churches of Christ in the
U.S.A., and used by permission.*

ISBN 087123 156 5

Printed in the United States of America

FOREWORD

God is so far away, so incomprehensible, so unfathomable. And then there is my life with all its earthly limitations, with its sadness and misery. Is it conceivable that there could be any link? To a great extent mankind today does not find this relation. Men resort to narcosis in order to overcome their sadness. Yet this leads them into an even greater sadness.

But this link is possible. In fact, it is even possible to have a very close contact—a personal relationship of love and child-like trust in the Father. What is actually incomprehensible to our human understanding is the fact: We are children of this holy and "distant" God, if we believe in Jesus Christ, His only Son. In Him, God the Father has drawn close to us. Through the sacrificial death of His Son He has granted us the privilege of being His children. Every day He wants to reveal His fatherly love to us in a new and different way. This statement of faith is certainly familiar to Christians—at least theoretically, but now it must be rediscovered and practised by us all.

This seems to me to be very important in our times when a nuclear war is threatening to bring disaster and destruction upon the earth. We will only experience His help and His comfort in difficult times if we learn how to trust our heavenly Father now. These short devotions for every day of the year are meant to teach us how to put our trust in the Father.

JANUARY

1

You need comfort, but do not have any. Yet, there is Someone who already has comfort ready for you. There is Someone who is deeply moved by all human suffering, and by yours also. It is not difficult for Him to comfort you. His love is so great that He always finds words and ways to comfort us. And His power to help is so great, that He always has an encouragement and a way for you. And if it does not come right away, it will come at just the right time!

2

You wonder where your path will lead you? You do not need to know. Just take the first step. After that God will show you the next step. Go step by step. One day you will realize that He has led you according to a wise plan, along a way which led to a glorious goal.

3

God is Love. He is merciful and filled with goodness. If you want to experience His mercy, be merciful to others. Then you will push open the door of His heart so that His mercy will flow over you.   *Matthew 5:7*

4

In His infinite love, God has prepared for us a precious gift of grace: contrition. People who are continually contrite are the richest people. They can always have a share in God's love, forgiveness, mercy and all His blessings of renewal. Whoever is often sorry for his sins will experience great pardon. God has promised grace to the penitent, humble hearts and not to the self-righteous, self-assured and self-satisfied. So strive for contrition, the most precious gift of all—the love of God is holding it ready for you.

An offer of grace: We are not only meant to receive the Father's love, forgiveness and goodness. We may also give the Father something in return. We may bring Him fruit by glorifying Him before men, for when people see our good works they will give the Father glory and honour.

Will we accept this offer of grace? Will we thank the Father by seeking to please Him? Will we dedicate ourselves to letting God prune our sinful nature so that fruit which is pleasing to Him will grow out of our lives? That would be a true sign of our gratitude to a Father who cannot bear to see anyone sad. *Matthew 5:16*

6

God wants His miraculous power and glory to be revealed before all the world. This happens through people who have faith in Him. Now He is waiting for this to happen through you. So take the risk of faith. Try to put your trust in Him in a hopeless situation. Then you will give God the glory, bring joy to His heart and magnify His name among men. And that will enrich and make you happy—and the miracles which you experience will strengthen your faith.

7

There is Someone who knows about our problems. He knows every worry. He knows how much anguish our problems and worries cause us and that is why He wants to help us. Could we have anything better? He wants to take care of what is troubling us. He wants to pave a way where we can no longer see a path. He wants to change the conditions which are a burden to us. He wants to send us help. Leave all the worrying to Him. Thank Him for taking the matter into His hands and helping you with the problems that are now weighing so heavily upon you and your heart will be filled with peace.

What could you be missing? There is Someone who is watching over you in love. He is concerned about you. He is the Father who loves you. Do not be concerned only with yourself or with your work or with your fellow men. Turn to your Lord who loves you, who is waiting for you. Think about Him often. Speak with Him. Love Him. Thank Him. Then you will no longer be alone. You will be united with Him. This union will make you strong and you will be comforted. You will have everything!

9

We have a heavenly Father who is almighty. Who will experience His mighty deeds? Those who believe Him. Faith is a power which can transform everything. It is not an empty faith, but rather faith in the living Lord, who has power to help and proves it to those who trust in Him. Therefore, have faith in Him when you are in despair, and the storm will be calmed. Believe in Him when you are afraid and your fears will subside. Believe—and you will experience miracles.

10

Is the burden which God has laid upon you too heavy to bear? Perhaps it is too heavy, because you are not willing to pick it up and to bear it step by step. Time and again you take it into your own hands. You look at your cross over and over again and weigh it to see whether you can pick it up at all. But in such a manner you cannot carry it. Through this process you will only come to self-pity and the burden will become almost unbearable. Willingly take the cross upon your back and you will experience that you can carry it. It comes from the Father's hands. He has weighed it out for you in love. It can never be an ounce too heavy.

Trust in the goodness of the Father, even when He leads you along paths of chastisement which hurt! It is especially during such times that God is fatherly disposed to His child. He is doing the best thing for you when He chastises you, for He is preparing you for heaven. Can there be anything greater than a love which prepares you for heaven, that is, which will make you happy forever? This begins here on earth when you are willing to accept chastisement.

12

God alone is the Creator! This is what creation declares. That means, however: It is not we men who are the creators of the universe. We are creatures and not lords. We are dependent upon God. Who ever does not love Him resists dependence. He wants to be free. He wants to determine his own life. He wants to rule. But whoever loves Him rejoices over this dependence, as a child is happy to be dependent upon his father whom he needs. This dependence ties the bond of love even tighter.

Therefore, affirm this dependence upon God the Father as His child and you will really be "the child of God" and experience the wealth and blessings of being His child. You will experience how blessed it is to be loved, led and cared for by God the Father.

13

Let us rejoice that our lives are being led. The hand of God is leading and guiding us according to a wise, eternal plan. His wisdom is leading us day by day straight forward towards the goal. Do not oppose His guidance. Otherwise you will destroy a plan full of glory for your life. Commit yourself to His will, even when it is difficult and incomprehensible for you. Thus, your way will end in a goal filled with joy and bliss for eternity.

You have been disappointed by people in whom you had placed your hope—especially because they are Christians. However God has sent you this disappointment, because He wants to attain something. Every hope which you place in people should come to naught so that you place your hope and trust in God alone.

God is the only One who does not disappoint us. People will always disappoint us more or less, because they are sinners. Even the Church of Jesus Christ is only a poor "manger" into which the treasure of the Gospel has been laid. It is this treasure that you should seek. It will remain eternally. It will never become less precious. Rather the more we come to know it, the more precious it will be to us, like our Lord Jesus Christ.

The love of God had a reason for sending you this disappointment. Let it accomplish its purpose in your heart: Be even more grateful that God never disappoints you. Turn to Him and love Him even more. And out of this love for God, learn to love what He loves also, the poor in spirit, the sinners.

15

The love of God the Father can never be comprehended in all eternity. He has been hurt and insulted by us. We have tortured His only Son with our sin and have martyred Him. What is God's answer to our disgraceful actions? God accepts us as His children through Jesus Christ. He loves and cares for us. He is opening heaven for us so that we may enter into His glory.

Still we dare to be incomprehensibly ungrateful and proud. Time and again we rebel against God. We accuse Him when we do not understand His actions and leadings. We think that He is being hard on us. Let us not be surprised if our relationship to God is disturbed, if we do not receive any help or comfort. God only gives grace to the humble.

Which power is greater? Earthly power (including nuclear power) or the heavenly power of God, who has created all earthly power? Logically the answer must be the power of the Creator. Therefore, trust in God, to whom everything is subject. Trust in His love. His power to help is stronger than all the powers of destruction.

17

When we judge or strike out against those who cause us difficulty, we are actually striking out against God Himself, because people who annoy us are His instruments. God is sending them to us in His wise plan to make us humble and teach us how to love. So humble yourself beneath the loving hand of God. Accept the behaviour of your difficult neighbour as His doing and you will share in the blessing which God has intended to give you through this.

18

God the Father is worthy of our love. Our love is important to Him. He gives a great deal for our love. Time and again He calls us to love Him and promises that He will love us in return. Yes, He wants to make His home in our hearts. He wants to visit you, if you love Him. What a visit! Incomprehensible grace and honour! Do not frivolously throw it away. Give God your love. You ask: How should I do that? Jesus gives you the answer: "He who has my commandments and keeps them, he it is who loves me." It is not a matter of feeling. It is simply a matter of being obedient to His commandments, above all His commandment of love: Love which bears all things, suffers all things, and does not become bitter. Therefore, whoever strives daily to keep His commandments will experience the Father's love most. *John 14:21, 24. 1 Corinthians 13*

Once—perhaps it was only yesterday—you experienced that God answered prayer, that God helped you in your difficulties, that He brought you through all your sorrow. Once—perhaps it was only yesterday—when you were very sad you experienced that He comforted you, that He did not let you be tempted beyond your strength. Do you think that the God of yesterday is not the same as the God of today? Believe that when "Jesus Christ is the same yesterday, today and for ever," then God, your Father, is also the same in all eternity. He will take care of you today also. He cannot tempt you, today either, beyond your strength. He will carry you through. Cling to that in trust and you will overcome all difficulties, in faith in the One whose power and love is the same today.

20

God has given you a great present. He has given you eyes which not only see what is visible: He has given you eyes of faith which can also see the invisible things, behind the scenes. And these are the very things which determine the visible world. Whoever uses his eyes of faith will be able to discover the secret of the love of God in his own life and in the life of mankind.

Then we will not only see the tribulation, but we will also see the glory which tribulation brings about. Then we will not only see our sin, but we will also see the victory of Jesus, which seeks realization in our lives. Then we will not only see our own life and the lives of others as a muddle, but we will see the wise and wonderful plan of God which stands behind it. Then we will not only see the darkness spreading over the earth, but we will also see the dawning of the kingdom of Jesus Christ. So look at the invisible, look at the great promises of God, and your life will be transformed.

God the Father loves us and wants to speak with us. He wants to reveal Himself to us and to impart Himself to us. However, He is the Holy One. To encounter Him means taking one's shoes off. It means separating ourselves for certain periods of time from people or relationships, from all activity in everyday life and becoming quiet inside. It means waiting for God to speak. Whoever does this will have encounters with God, which will change his life and give Him power and authority for ministry in the kingdom of God.

22

People who have something to expect are excited and joyful. They are never bored. There is something exciting about waiting because love is involved. So wait for the coming of God, your Father. He is coming, because His love continually draws Him to us. He always brings something wonderful with Him, a word for us, a joy, a present. Look for Him and your heart will become alive and happy.

23

The verse: "the Lord is compassionate and merciful" applies to the life of Job. The Lord pitied Job. God as the Heavenly Father suffered with His servant Job when he had to go through such difficult sufferings. Whoever bears the sufferings of another, seeks ways to prepare for him a good ending. So at the end God bestowed more good things upon Job than he had had before. He reinstated his fortune. That is an eternal law of the love of God in His relationship to His chosen ones. Therefore, wait for the gracious ending of your suffering and you will experience that later God will do more good things for you than ever before.   *James 5:11*

God calls Himself our Father in Jesus Christ. Above all, He is concerned that we love Him, because a Father expects His children to love Him. We were created and redeemed to love God. Whoever loves God above all things has found the eternal purpose of his life. For time and eternity he has complete abundance and is filled with joy.

25

Pray daily like the disciples: "Lord, increase our faith!" There is one thing which we continually lack: strong faith. But in order to carry out the commissions which God gives us, faith is completely necessary. In all our work and activity—yes, even in praying, everything depends upon our faith. Faith determines whether your activity and your prayers will bring fruit. Perhaps you pray a great deal to God and even pray the same thing over and over again. However, if you do not count on God's having prepared help for you and you do not await this help, then nothing will happen. If you are lacking faith, then ask for it and count on God's answering your plea. He will instill faith within you. God will bless this first step of faith and give you additional prayers of faith.

Luke 17:5

26

You are about to resign. You think you cannot fight any longer. You think it is all in vain. However, as far as God's love is concerned there is no "in vain". This is what the cross on Calvary shows us. Here a "battle fought in vain" led to the most glorious victory. Therefore, God is calling to you: 'Resigning means losing the battle. But continuing to fight means winning. So, take up the battle again, and you will win. The cross of Jesus is over you as the sign of victory.'

"Sing unto the Lord!" Even on the days which are loaded with work? Yes, especially then. When we sing, we bring heaven down to us. God inclines Himself to us when we sing praises to Him, and He will fill our work with His Spirit. Then our work will be blessed and prosperous. And we will become strong enough to tread the difficulties under our feet. Thus, our work will bring eternal fruit, because it has been done in God. *Psalm 96:1*

28

A true child of the Father knows what it is to be astonished. A child is astonished about what the Father can do and what He knows. Awe and reverence grow out of this astonishment. He who recognizes his own limitations and destitution most clearly will be able to be most astonished about the omnipotence, wisdom and love of God, draw near to Him in holy reverence and praise Him in adoration. Can we still be astonished about the greatness, glory and love of God? Can we worship Him in awe? It is a sign of the true children of God. Do we have it?

29

God Himself tells us that He rejoices in doing good things for us, His children. However, He often has to wait until we are ready to receive the good things. Otherwise we would trample them with our dirty feet. First He has to prepare us so that we are in the position to receive the good properly. Only then will it provide us true joy and blessing. Instead of being defiant when you have to wait, commit yourself to being chastened and to being prepared to receive His gifts correctly. Then you will receive them even more quickly. It all depends upon you, when God can give you His gifts. *Jeremiah 32:41*

How can you overcome the fear of an approaching nuclear war? Meditate on the love of God the Father. Whoever looks at His love will be comforted. Love always has a way to help and protect, even in the greatest affliction. It can even command fire not to burn. Remember the angel who was sent to help the friends of Daniel in the fiery furnace. God has given us a promise which at all times is valid for His children: He will be with us in times of trouble. He says: "When you pass through the waters I will be with you; and through the rivers, they shall not overwhelm you; when you walk through fire you shall not be burned, and the flame shall not consume you." God will be near you in the greatest times of tribulation in order to help you. May that be sufficient comfort for you. *Isaiah 43:2*

31

God loves the small and lowly who let themselves be corrected. But God turns away from those who accuse others in their hearts or with words. They bear the traits of the accuser, of the haughty Lucifer, the enemy of God. If you wish to be loved by God, be your own accuser. Do not take sides against others. Only take sides against yourself. Then God will be on your side. He will give you His love and will intercede on your behalf.

FEBRUARY 1

God is a true Father. Discipline and punishment of His children belong to His nature. His love cannot stand by and watch people heading for disaster and death. Therefore, He often resorts to admonishing and punishing us. Otherwise we would not listen to Him. Listen to His admonishments and you will be spared many punishments and blows of judgment.

Rejoice! When the times are turbulent and wars begin to rage, rejoice, because you are really sitting in the shelter of the Most High. He has promised this and He keeps His word. Thank God for promising to prove His might on behalf of His children in times of great affliction and war. By giving thanks and rejoicing now, you will receive the great strength which you will need in times of trouble and to face all the fears you have in anticipation of these times. Through the strength born out of thinking and rejoicing you will overcome. *Psalm 91:1, 2*

3

You are restless. You have many worries. Yet, you cannot solve your problems and difficulties by yourself. Your own restless thinking and wishing makes you weak and weary. It clogs the channel of your heart through which God wants to let His help flow. Leave everything to God. Let all your thoughts, worries and plans come to rest. Rest in God and in His reign, in the knowledge that He will act! Then you will experience that "in quietness and in trust shall be your strength." So choose this way and He will help you.

Isaiah 30:15

4

Whoever wants to know what a loving Father God is should picture in spirit the city of God. Out of great love, God has prepared a heavenly creation full of glory and perfect beauty to be the eternal dwelling place of those who belong to Him. The Father wants to see His children happy. That is why He has prepared heaven, the city of God, for their eternal home, where they can live in bliss. Therefore, in days of suffering think of the love of the Father, which has prepared a heaven full of glory. Then all earthly sufferings will lose their power of sadness.

Waiting often belongs to the plan of God—waiting until our problems have reached a climax. That is how God worked with His disciples when they were in great distress during the storm on the sea. God could have calmed the first wave. But then the disciples would never have become acquainted with the power and glory of Jesus Christ. Think about this whenever the waves around you get higher and higher. God is letting them rise so high—as He did for the children of Israel at the crossing of the Red Sea,—so that He can prove His miraculous power and can glorify His name.

Wait for Him to reveal His glory and to perform miracles in your needs and you will experience the truth of this verse: "If you would believe, you would see the glory of God."   *John 11:40*

6

Who will live to please the Father? Who will live to bring Him joy? Only the child, who like the Prodigal Son, daily turns around and comes home to the Father and says to Him: "Father, I have sinned." In love and joy the Father's heart will incline itself to those who repent. Be such a child of the Father and His pleasure will rest upon you.

7

God wants to rescue people and nations from their misfortune by His chastising hand. However, misfortune and judgment are the consequences of sin. Therefore, the judgments of God call people to forsake their sinful ways; He desires to bring them salvation. Do not resist God's discipline, because it contains a great offer of grace and salvation. Grace lies hidden in judgment—for you also.

Because God is Love, He is concerned that His children love. How do I love Him? Love God by loving your neighbour as yourself. Love God by saying NO to every sin. Love God by reconciling yourself with every person just as He reconciled Himself with you in His only Son. Love God by giving up your self-love and your own will. Love your God, who constantly bestows His blessings upon you, by dedicating yourself to Him wholeheartedly. He will repay your love richly.

9

We of the atomic age are seeking security as no other previous generation. In the time of great tribulation only he will be secure who is already at home in the heart of God. Whoever can now say in all his troubles: "The Lord is good, a stronghold in the day of trouble," will one day in great tribulation experience that the Lord will prove Himself to him, just as he had believed Him all the years. So let us take advantage of the time we still have and practice living in the security of His heart! Then we will be given grace to do it also in the time of trouble. *Nahum 1:7*

10

In the Word of God it is written: "For my father and my mother have forsaken me, but the Lord will take me up." When human support and earthly assistance, in every form, is taken from us, the power of God will become most effective. A person who puts his trust in crutches cannot be taught how to walk. Therefore, the Lord is calling to us: Throw away your crutches so that My power can be effective for you. When you go your way in My strength, it will become filled with victory and joy. Do not put any limitation on My power. *Psalm 27:10*

Whoever is in suffering, in need, temptation, and sorrow of sin is among the first who will come home to the heart of God. A child in tears belongs in the Father's arms. They are wide open for him.

12

You think that God is fighting against you. But, believe that whenever it seems as though God is fighting against you, He is really fighting for you. For He is and will remain your Father, who loves you. But sometimes He does seem to place Himself in the position of an enemy, as He did with Jacob, in order to challenge you to a persevering battle of faith. Like Jacob you should say over and over again: "I will not let you go, until you bless me." Through such a wrestling match of faith God wants to make you a victor—a bearer of blessing to whom He can entrust great commissions.
Genesis 32:26

13

The heavenly Father has always intended to give His children joy here on earth. We do not have to wait until we are in heaven. He wants to give His children the treasure in the field, the pearl of the kingdom of heaven and open up the secret of festive heavenly joy here on earth.

Therefore do not prefer the festivals and joys of this earth to the gifts of God, mistrusting and questioning whether God really wants to give you true happiness and fulfillment in your life. When your life grows dark and earthly joys grow dim, you would then be desperately poor. Take the risk and forego earthly joys for the sake of heavenly, eternal joys. You will not regret it. You will be overjoyed. Do not wait until the doors are closed before you turn to your Father in complete trust. Then it will be too late.

You know that God is your Father. However, it seems as though you no longer have any access to Him. You think that your failures are too great in the sight of God and man. But, God is challenging you: Say YES to your failures. That is honest, that is courageous, humble. This YES is the key to the door of the Father's heart. It will open it and a stream of grace will pour into you. A confession of your fault also opens the door to the heart of your neighbour, whom you have wronged. What grace God offers us!

15

God suffers as a Father, because He is often excluded by people, even by His own. We claim help and solicitude from everyone else, but we often no longer count on God and His actual intervention and help. However, he who has not learned how to count on God in his everyday life will not be able to do it in times of trouble either, when all human help breaks down. He will not see any way out. Therefore we have to learn to count on God's help today.

16

As far as our lives are concerned, we are construction workers, not architects. We do not have to plan for our whole life. The Architect of our life, who is holding the plan in His hands, is God Himself. We are not being tossed about by a power of fate. God is leading our lives according to a wonderful plan along a way corresponding to our strength and talents.

Therefore do not prevent God from being the Architect of your life. Desire to be and do what is fitting for you: To be obedient to His leading and to place the stones according to His plan, day by day, in the edifice of your life—and a wonderful structure will evolve.

Jesus brings us good news: Sinners, poor creatures, may call the almighty God, who created a universe of glory and greatness, their Father. Are we conscious of this privilege? Profit from this privilege of having an almighty Lord for your Father. Make use of this privilege through childlike prayer and trust, and you will receive help whenever you need it.

18

God calls Himself your Father. He is waiting for you, His child, to love Him. The Father is looking for your love—the love of His children is His joy. But you will only be a joy to Him, in so far as you "love God above all". Then you will commit to Him all the things that you are attached to—whether they be people or things. Then, out of love, you will sacrifice to Him whatever your heart clings to. Then you will bring joy to the heart of God, and in loving the joy of God will make you rich and happy.

19

The Father's love has thought up an abundant reward for all His children's tears. He Himself will wipe away every tear from their eyes. He will take them into His arms. He will embrace them, just as Jesus depicted the father's love in the parable of the Prodigal Son. After this slight momentary affliction, He wants to give us an eternal weight of glory beyond all comparison. Jubilation and exultation will take hold of us. He wants to repay us, without end, for our sufferings. Full of joy He wants to show us the harvest of our days on earth. Our thoughts should be directed towards this goal. Then our greatest sufferings will seem small to us.

Revelation 21:4. II Corinthians 4:17

God is Love! May this fact be sufficient for you. Do not try to understand God when His leadings seem incomprehensible. Rather, humble yourself beneath them. Then you will become wise, and God's heart will be opened for you. Through humble love you will be able to comprehend deeply the nature of His love although your intellect cannot understand His actions. So humble yourself beneath the powerful hand of God and you will find peace and rest in the will of God through all His incomprehensible leadings.

21

You know that it is grace which has given you the privilege of prayer. However, it is a matter of praying in faith, in firm faith that God will really help. Let your faith come alive. Do not only bring your petitions, but pray like this: 'I thank You for already having planned the help for me, for already having a solution to my problem, because Jesus' victory over my sin has already been won.' Such prayer has promise. It moves the arm of God so that the problem must yield before His omnipotence. Make use of this opportunity. In this prayer of thanksgiving you will become happy and strengthened. When your pleas to the heavenly Father are embedded in thanksgiving and faith then they will certainly be answered.

22

What is the highest goal that God has set for your life? God arranges everything in our life in order to teach us how to love. For through His beloved Son He has redeemed us for the most beautiful image, for the image of His love. Now can you understand God's actions, especially when He puts difficult people in your life? This will certainly help you.

When you cannot get rid of sadness and melancholy, say this one sentence aloud: 'Yes, Father, I want my cross.' This will make your heavy burden lighter. A commitment of our will to God's working in our lives has power to transform the human heart. Then your problems lose their bitterness.

24

God loves us. That is why He makes every effort to make the day of His Son's return the day of our joy and delight. That is what Holy Scripture says. Who will have a share in this joy? Those who suffer here with Christ. However, we will not have to wait for the second coming before He gives us this joy. No, we are told: "Rejoice in so far as you share Christ's sufferings!" In the name of God, the Apostle is challenging us to rejoice in the midst of suffering. He speaks of suffering for Jesus' sake as a special privilege. "You are privileged to share in the suffering of Jesus, in His disgrace." Why is it a privilege? Because this suffering is the way to the abundant joy that our Father, who cannot bear to see anyone sad, wants to give us.

When God counts you worthy to be misunderstood, excluded, discriminated against and scorned by others, say: 'Thank You for counting me worthy to suffer for Your name's sake.' Then joy will enter your heart.   *I Peter 4:13*

25

God, as the Father of love, is a Lord who distributes gifts lavishly: an abundance of beauty in nature—an abundance of gifts and talents for His children. He is a rich Giver. Are you poor, because you have a small heart that does not expect anything big from Him?

You are wondering how your problems can be solved. You have considered all visible possibilities. However, the solution will come from another source. It will come from the invisible world, from the reality of God. Count on it. All at once God will become real to you and you will notice His presence.

I am missing a great deal. I am lacking everything. That is why there is no more help for me. This is what you ascertain. However, as far as God your Father is concerned, it does not matter whether you are missing much or little. On the contrary, the more you are lacking, the more He can demonstrate His miraculous power. So boast: 'God will give me what I am missing, simply because I am missing a great deal.' Such faith will experience a transformation of circumstances.

God is love. That is why He is so concerned that His children come to love. He knows that if we love, everything will fall into place. That is why He says to us: 'Love, as I have loved you—love, without seeking love in return. Bear those who do evil to you, as your Father bears the evil ones. Return good for the evil which has been done to you in word or deed. Love others with a love that is prepared to bear everything, never becoming tired and always thinking the best of him.'

This love is victorious. It has power, because it streams out of God's heart into ours. May it be our deepest desire to attain this love. Everyone can receive it, because this promise is valid for everyone: "Ask, and you will receive."

John 16:24

A nuclear war is threatening us—destruction, fall-out, disaster. People ascertain: There is no more help left. However, His own have a pledge which guarantees them help for these times also: "Our God is a God of salvation; and to God, the Lord, belongs escape from death." Jesus, as the Prince of Life, is stronger than all the powers of destruction and death. He can rescue us from death in a wonderful manner and when He calls us to Him, He will gloriously lead us through the gate of death, for His very presence overcomes death.

Psalm 68:20

MARCH 1

Perhaps you are grumbling in your heart that God does not give you any comfort or help in your sufferings. However, your grumbling, complaining and protesting against the leadings of God and against the burden of your cross are erecting a dam to block the blessings of God. So the comfort and help which He has intended to give you cannot flow through into your heart. Commit yourself completely to God by accepting God's way and His working in you. Then the way will be free so that the blessing of suffering can stream forth into your life.

2

God knows our hearts. He knows that we have so little confidence, that is why He gives us promises. They are valid. He does not deceive His children, whom He loves. So for times of great trouble He has said to those who know His name: "I will protect him." Stand firmly upon His pledge and take your refuge in Him. Then you will experience that His hand, which has created the world, is stronger than all other powers, even stronger than nuclear weapons and the forces of nature. His hands can hold them back.

Psalm 91:14

You have fallen down. You are dirty. You no longer dare to step into God's presence. He seems to be so far away from you. But it is exactly now that the Father is waiting for you. He waits for the child who has fallen down, as a mother waits for her child who has got dirty so that she can wash him. He wants to cleanse you in the blood of His Son. So come!

4

Are you lacking faith? Your faith will be fired by God's nature. Prayerfully, pronounce the characteristics of God: 'You are almighty, all-wise, all-loving, merciful, ever-present.' Say with Job: "I know that thou canst do all things, and that no purpose of thine can be thwarted." Or join him in praising God "who does great things beyond understanding, and marvelous things without number. Your faith will be set a flame when you proclaim the strength and power of God. Then you will experience that those who believe in the power of the almighty God will never lack anything.   *Job 42:2. Job 9:10*

5

The kingdom of heaven, with all its blessings in the way of security, holy carefreeness and blessed love, belongs to children. However, being a child of God must be practiced through lowliness and humility in everyday life. God's children ask people to forgive them. They humble themselves before others. They are willing to take the last place. They are willing not to be recognized. They let others correct them like a child. Those who do such things will experience the truth of this promise: The kingdom of heaven belongs to children. Here on earth they will taste something of the kingdom of heaven.   *Matthew 19:14*

God, our heavenly Father, is the only true Father, whose heart is only goodness and love. Everyone who trusts in Him will experience this. But whoever mistrusts God and thinks that He will not do good things for us and will not help us will receive no help. Mistrust destroys the relationship of love which the Father has with us and binds His hands. We will only experience what we believe.

7

The heart of God our Father is laden with love. It is written that He wants to give us more good things than we ask for and more than we can understand. Indeed, we shall "fear and tremble because of all the good and all the prosperity He provides." He wants to make us excessively happy. It is God's concern that our hearts be filled with great joy. Therefore, Jesus says: "These things I have spoken to you that your joy may be full."

Do we believe that God wants to give us this excessive joy? Only then will we be able to partake of this joy which will express itself in astonishment, yes, in fear and trembling because of all the good things that the Father in heaven does for us. Ask in the name of Jesus for this gift of joy which God has prepared for you. God is waiting for you to ask so that He can fulfill your request.

Jeremiah 33:9. John 15:11

8

God, the almighty and powerful God, likes to do great things. But He can seldom do great things, because we are standing in His way with our own greatness, importance, conceit and self-confidence. Therefore, He is calling to us: 'Humble yourselves, become small and lowly!' He only uses the small ones, who do not stand in His way, to perform His great deeds.

Why do we get so upset? Why do we get angry? Why do we worry? By being angry and worrying, we prevent God from working in our lives and blessing our work. It is our own will, which wants to get something done quickly. Our will has not been surrendered to God.

Stop whenever you sense your heart becoming angered or irritated. Become quiet before God. Commit your will to Him and say: 'The way You do it, the way You lead me, the way You prevent me from doing something is good. You have planned everything well. I trust You. I commit myself to Your will. You have redeemed me from my own will and from my worries.' Then you will experience the peace of God streaming into your heart, and your work will be blessed.

10

You are plagued by bitter thoughts, by accusations against your fellow men. You cannot understand why God lets them do you so much wrong. However, God wants to help you and He is telling you: 'Your thoughts are wandering in the wrong direction. You are unhappy, because you have bound yourself to Satan, the accuser, who always makes us melancholy.'

Instead of accusing others, accuse yourself, because you cause God trouble every day with your sins, because you have caused so many other people distress. Thank the Lord for being so kind to you in spite of your faults and then be kind to your neighbour. Thank God, in His love for wanting to free you from your accusations, by showing you your own sins. Now the hour has come for God to help you, cleanse you, free you from reproaches and fill your heart with peace. Accept His help.

You say that you have not received any comfort on your way of the cross. Is it perhaps due to the fact that you do not bend down low enough beneath your cross? Perhaps you have not yet said with your whole heart: 'Put it on me, my Father, I want to carry it. I need it.' The prayer, 'Yes, Father', has great power. It will make your cross light for you. It will bring the Father's love to you. Therefore, say this one word 'Yes', and you will receive comfort.

12

God must judge us, because He loves us. Yet, whenever He has to judge, His sympathetic heart weeps. So Jesus wept, when He spoke of the destruction of Jerusalem. God's heart shares all our sufferings with us. It is hard for Him to punish us. Thus, how easy it is for us, to change God's intention to punish us! When we turn away from ways which grieve God and man, and when we begin to cry over our sin, Jesus' tears will be stopped and the chastisement of God will be turned into grace.

13

Jesus teaches us to pray: "Thy will be done!" Actually this is to our ultimate advantage. With this plea we exclude the possibility that our will be done. Our will is so limited and we are so inclined to err. It can only lead us into misfortune. But, if God's will is done, it is the will of perfect wisdom, of love. God alone knows what is good for man, whereas we do not know what is good for us. So pray with the complete surrender of your will and desires: "God, Thy will be done!" Surrender yourself to His will completely, and you will have chosen the best portion for your life. With great love God will lead you to the most glorious goal.

Keep your quiet times with God. Give Him more time. Abiding in God's presence cannot be replaced by anything. In the presence of God you will become strong. Through His presence you will be transformed. Seek His presence and it will solve everything that you cannot solve by yourself.

15

There are three little words that contain the solution to all your problems. They are, "Trust in God". That means believing that God is really almighty and is really a Father full of love, always prepared to help. Trust, and the first step toward the solution of your difficulties has been taken. The second will follow. With your own eyes you will see that in His time He will transform your sorrow into joy.

16

When you are sad and in distress, God, our Father, calls to you: 'Why are you cast down, and why are you so disquieted? I have a way to help you. Trust Me with confidence, that is, wait and expect help. It will surely come. Yes, I tell you now that you will be joyful and give thanks for that which is oppressing you so much today.' Therefore, begin now to pray: 'I thank You that I can go forward confidently in expectation of help.' And you will indeed go forward confidently, going forth to meet the day of help.

17

God, who is Love, gives us a ray of light every day no matter how dark it may be: a solution, a help, a greeting, an encouragement. Look for the light. It is there. And you will see the way illuminated before you.

Whoever has a wish goes to the one who loves him most. This is the person who will most likely fulfill his wishes. No one loves you as much as God, who calls Himself your Father. Come to Him with your wishes. Come to Him like a child, who begs from his father until he has fulfilled his request. When we ask Him in a childlike and trusting manner with humble, obedient hearts, we will attain everything except what would be harmful for us. Be a child, and as a child you will receive present after present from your Father.

19

There is one thing that is certain for times of tribulation. For the sake of His own honour, God, the Father, will glorify His name. He is called "wonderful" and He wants to magnify His name through wondrous miracles and signs of His help. When anguish reaches its peak, He will prove that He is greater than the anguish, that wind and waves and the powers of destruction are all subject to Him. He will bear wonderfully His elect, who call to Him night and day, through all distress. *Isaiah 9:6. Luke 18:7*

20

You ask why God does not answer your prayers? There are obstacles to prayer. God sees that we often misuse His gifts, For instance, we misuse the gift of forgiveness by not forgiving others. Thereby, we place an obstacle in the way of the other gifts of God. When God does not answer us, we should first ask whether we have put up an obstacle to prayers. Then, strive to remove it through godly sorrow, confession and repentance and you will experience that the way will be free and your prayers can rise up to God.

Do you want to understand the love of God, your Father? Listen to what He says: "I will remember their sin no more!" God has forgotten our debts of sin, even the gravest ones, whenever we have repented of them. However, there is something which He will never forget: The smallest deeds and sacrifices which we brought to Him out of love. Who can comprehend this love? When you consider that God acts like this, it will give you the courage to trust in His love in darkest hours.   *Jeremiah 31:34*

22

Ways of preparation and chastisement are often the answer to our prayers that God transform us into His image and let us reach the goal of glory. Now the Lord is leading you towards the goal which you have ultimately desired. You would not reach it going an easier way. Otherwise God would have chosen it. So, love the way which God is leading you, because it is the fulfilment of your prayer and it will bring you glory.

23

Do not look at your needs and impossibilities. Do not stop there. Remember: God is a Father. He is love. He has much better things in store for you. The difficulties are not the destiny God intended for you, but rather in every case a solution to your problems, joy and glory.

24

You are perplexed. Behold, there is Someone near you, who can advise you. You are helpless. Behold, He speaks: "I am here!" He will come to help you. It is your Lord and your God, your Father. Trust in Him, the ever-present Father, who helps you—and you will be helped.

We are afraid of the threatening destruction. Therefore, we look for a power that is stronger than the nuclear weapons and radioactive fall-out. We are looking for something to protect us from these things. If we knew this power, our problems would be solved. This power exists. He is the Lord who has made heaven and earth. He holds nuclear energy in His hands. Through His Son, He is calling to us: "Behold I have given you authority over all the power of the enemy." If you drink any deadly thing, it will not hurt you. His Word is valid. *Luke 10:19. Mark 16:18*

26

The sign of a poor child is that he always comes to his father to tell him his wishes, to beg something from him. The sign of a true father is that his child's begging in faith makes him happy. These are the characteristics of a true relationship between father and child. God longs to have this relationship with us. Assume this position of a child and you will experience the abundance of fatherly love, fatherly help and fatherly gifts. Be a genuine child towards God. Then the kingdom of heaven with all its treasures will belong to you.

27

God, the Father, sees His children who have voluntarily chosen to go the way of the cross out of love for His Son and who enter poverty, lowliness and many different types of suffering for Jesus' sake. He will never overlook them in their suffering. Time and again He will give such children joy and encouragement. When you are bearing a heavy cross, expect these things. Whoever expects refreshment will receive it. Whoever closes his heart resentfully resists God's blessings and His good gifts.

God is Love. One of the characteristics of love is faithfulness. He will never leave you. He will never disappoint you. He will guide you and sustain you up to the end. However, He is asking you for your love. He is asking you: 'When you can no longer understand Me, when you have to go difficult paths of suffering, then keep your trust in Me and your loyalty to Me as a sign of your love.'

29

You complain, because so few people love you, because there are so many who are not interested in knowing anything about you. They reject you. This is not God's intention. He, who is Love, wants to make our lives rich and happy. That is why God wants to solve your problems. He will show you the way. Love can even overcome people who are against us or hostile towards us. They will be conquered by a love, which commits itself to them, which does not repay evil with evil, but rather blesses them and does them good. Go this way, which the love of God offers to you, and you will harvest love.

30

In the face of threatening catastrophes and coming wars God speaks like a Father to you, His small, fearful child: "No evil shall befall you, no scourge come near your tent." Yet you wonder how that could be possible in the midst of the great chaos. God will protect you through the mighty, strong angels whom He has ready for you. But you want to pose another question, the question of death. If you die during this time, angels will carry you home and the presence of Jesus and His love will cover you so that no evil will befall you. This is what the future holds for you.   *Psalm 91:10*

As a true Father, God gives His children promises which He pledges to fulfill. Can we possibly assume that God could ever break His pledge and not let us experience the fulfillment of His promises? That is impossible. God is Truth, and He is Love. Truly, He does not give us promises in order to disappoint us, but in order to assure us of His help. Therefore, cling to His promises—hang on to them, and help will come.

APRIL **1**

It is difficult for you to accept God's will. God's will seems hard to you. It seems to be ruining your life. Whenever God shatters a life's dream, He wants to build something new on the foundation of a broken heart. He will give you something greater, something more wonderful, for God is Love. He never deprives us of anything which really would have been best for our lives. He only seeks to strike the impurities in our life, so that He can build up in a much more wonderful way, that which lies shattered to pieces before our eyes. He will fulfill the deepest longings of our hearts. Expect that, and you will be able to accept the will of God. Then you will find complete comfort.

2

When we are despondent and on the verge of despair, when there is no help in sight, let us say a verse from the Holy Scriptures out loud: "God is our refuge and strength, a very present help in trouble." God can help, because He is the Almighty and God wants to help, because He is Love, and love always has to help. Therefore, we can be sure that He will help us. Only if we say that He cannot help us, will we prevent Him from doing so. *Psalm 46:1*

The angels of God are not without souls. We read in the Holy Scriptures that they rejoice over one sinner who repents. How much more will God the Father rejoice! Therefore, it lies within the realm of our possibilities to bring joy to the heart of the heavenly Father. Usually we cannot do this. We fall down so often, grieve Him through our sinning and cause Him so much work and trouble. However, for every person even the worst sinner, there is a way to bring joy to the heart of the heavenly Father: the way of repentance.   *Luke 15:7*

4

God's heart is filled with love towards us. He continually urges us to be childlike and bring our wishes to Him. He is a Father and He rejoices whenever He can make us happy and give us things. Now He is standing beside you saying: 'Behave like a real child towards Me. Do not be shy. Day by day bring your wishes, large and small, to Me, your Father.'— Jesus has promised us that the Father will do good things for us when we ask Him. Try it out!   *Matthew 7:11*

5

Through the past we have learned that God thinks of His children more than ever during times of trouble and sends them help. This should teach us a lesson for the coming time of destruction. The Lord expects His children to begin now to rely upon His Word: "Thou hast been my help, and in the shadow of thy wings I sing for joy." Pray again and again: 'I have a Helper. He is my God and my Lord. In times of misfortune I will not only be hid beneath His wings, but I will also sing for joy.' This declaration of faith will comfort you.   *Psalm 63:7*

You think you can no longer bear the burden that has been placed upon you. But listen! The Father wants to comfort you as His child: The dark valley is almost over. Soon bright beams of joy and bliss will be waiting for you. You will laugh as much as you have cried. "Blessed are you that weep now, for you shall laugh." Live in expectation of the hour when your weeping will turn to laughter. This hour will come and in all eternity your laughter will never cease. This hour will come while you are still on earth—and perhaps it will be tomorrow. Wait in anticipation! *Luke 6:21*

7

God works wonders. This is part of His nature, because His name is "Wonderful". He is the Almighty. He can create new life. He can do things that are impossible for man. However, today, as long ago, our unbelief hinders Him from displaying His miraculous power. This is painful for God and also for us. He is waiting for people who will turn to Him when they are in distress and sing His praises: "Thou art the God who workest wonders." When you confess God as the God who works wonders and when you praise His power, you will experience His wonders in your life—but not otherwise. *Isaiah 9:6. Psalm 77:14*

8

Learn a song which has power to banish all fears and worries. It is the song of love for the Father. 'My Father, my dearest Father!' Who sings it? All the Christians who have really become children of the heavenly Father. They live in dependence upon God, trusting, small and lowly like children. They are at home in the Father's house where this song is constantly sung. Let it be your song. It will banish fear and worry.

You are torturing yourself by constantly thinking about
yourself. You are such a difficult person. You cannot accept
yourself. But God, who has created you and who loves you,
wants to help you. He is showing you the way: Accept yourself as you are, and God will turn you into what you are not
yet. He gives grace to the humble.

10

If we want God to answer our prayers, we have to pray the
prayers He promised to answer. Jesus tells us what one of
these prayers is. It is the prayer in His name. Say the name
of Jesus to God the Father. Jesus is His beloved Son.

His name is a key which opens the Father's heart. Let Him
show you the concerns which can be claimed in Jesus'
name, because they are according to the spirit and will of
Jesus. Then God cannot resist your plea. The name of Jesus,
who has shed His blood for us, masters His heart. The
Father cannot deny the Son His pleas. Therefore, Jesus
says: "If you ask anything of the Father, he will give it to
you in my name." Do you ask like this? Then you will experience the fulfillment of your prayers.   *John 16:23*

11

God, the great and almighty Lord, does not perform His
miracles like a magician. He performs them as a Father, as
the Father of love. Love can only reveal itself to hearts
which are open and bring Him their requests in expectation
and complete trust. Love is tender. It does not force itself
upon us. Only he who has a childlike relationship of trust
to the Father will experience the miracles and great deeds
of God. But, whoever trusts will always experience them.

God is omnipresent and omnipotent. He rules the universe; He searches the depths. But His greatness is revealed by the fact that at the same time He thinks of the very smallest things. He has numbered every hair on our heads. Whoever has eyes to see the greatness of God, the greatness of the fatherly love in His consideration of the smallest details, has truly comprehended the nature and glory of God. Ask Him to give you such eyes. Then you will be able to see the traces of His great actions everywhere. Then you will know that He is leading you even in the smallest things.

13

The love of God is meant for the small and lowly, for the ones who do not think much of themselves, who do not want to receive attention and recognition, who reprove themselves and who are willing to be ignored. The Father comes to them with His comfort, help and goodness. The Father gives them all the good things that they pray for. So choose the way of the lowly. Become one of the little ones and you will have a share in His gifts.

14

Because God is Love and because He loves you, He wants you to show Him your love. In Spirit He shows you His Son who forsook the love of His Father and the glory of heaven out of love for us. Now God is asking you: 'How have you thanked Him? What have you forsaken for Him?' But do not only sacrifice your gifts to Him. Give Him yourself, your freedom, your wishes and desires, your whole heart and life. Such a sacrifice will bind you to God and will unite you with Him. Then you will have found the greatest treasure in heaven and on earth, and you will become a happy person.

A child cannot do everything that big people can do. He is dependent upon the help of grown-ups, and he expects them to help him. But he thinks it is just as natural that grown-ups send him here and there. He is completely at their disposal. He lets them correct him and punish him. Whoever is a child of God in this manner will experience what the Father in heaven has promised the small and the weak: His loving care, His aid, His miracles.

16

God your Father often leads you along difficult paths which you do not like. The time has come for you to learn a lesson: To learn to want what He wants. Whoever has learned this lesson, whoever can completely accept the will of God in every situation, has learned something which will fill his life with peace and joy. Even on the most difficult paths he will be happy and at peace, for he is resting in the will which is always the best will. When you are confronted with the small problems of life, practise praying: "Thy will be done!" Then you will be able to rest in God's will in times of deepest suffering. Then you will be victorious.

17

You are dejected. You cannot rejoice in God. Begin to write down a list of what God means to you. He is a God who helps. He is a Father who loves you, who always has thoughts of goodness. He is the great Perfecter, who will carry out His plan of glory for you to perfection. He is almighty and is offering you shelter and protection. He has given His only Son for your redemption. When you think of these things and praise God for them, your joy will be newly set afire and all melancholy and sadness will yield.

Whoever lets go of security and becomes completely dependent upon God will find out in difficult times how wise he was. Only security in God is lasting. God is the best insurance. His resources never give out. With God, at any time and in any situation, you can get everything you need. Give up your other securities.

19

As a child of the heavenly Father you cannot be bold enough in faith in His love and in His power. It is apparent that bold faith pleases God—He challenges us often to be bold. God rejoices over such faith, and He cannot disappoint those who boldly ask in faith—if they walk according to His commandments.

20

No one who feels poor, weak and miserable will be lost in the storms of affliction and war. The Father has arms which will carry everyone who is poor and weak. The one thing that He cannot do is let us fall into the abyss. Place yourself in the arms of the Father, and you will be securely hid. He will carry you through all storms.

21

God is holy and righteous. He is wrathful against sin and holds out His hand ready to strike the sinful and the fallen. However, He holds out His hand ready to help and save all who love Him and live according to His commandments. He is calling to them: "The souls of the righteous are in the hand of God, and there shall no torment touch them." Who will experience this in times of distress, war and judgment? Those who claim this pledge from the Lord.

Wisdom of Solomon 3:1

The Father never forgets those who suffer. They remind Him of the sufferings of His Son. Therefore, the Father always opens His heart to them in His abundant, merciful love. You can count on that!

23

What is the way to happiness? Complete commitment to God. That means the complete surrender of your will at every moment to the will of God. This is the foundation of all happiness. Whoever has completely committed His will to God's will and commits it over and over again is free from his own self-will which seeks to tear him to pieces and the worries which seek to oppress him. Instead of that he rests in the will of God, in the loving will of the Father, who has the very best plans for us. That makes him happy.

24

The nature of God is greatness, omnipotence and glory. For Him nothing is "impossible", even though there are many things that are impossible for us poor, weak men with our limited capabilities. Whenever we find an insoluble problem in our life or seem to be in a situation that has no way out, He wants us to experience that "with God all things are possible"—if we believe that He is able. God expects the "impossible" to set our faith on fire. That is why He leads us into such relationships and situations.

When we believe the pledges of God in our troubles and "hopeless" situations, we will experience how possible the impossible becomes. Barricaded roads are made free; people's hearts are transformed. The greater the hopelessness seems to be, the greater the Lord proves to be.   *Matthew 19:26*

You are crying bitter tears. Have you considered the fact that you are not forgotten now? The Father is watching you with mercy, and He has already planned help for you. Your suffering has touched His heart. He sees it. He already has comfort and help prepared for you. Believe this!

26

There is a fatherly heart which can never give a human soul up for lost, unless He loses His own identity. But that cannot be, for God is eternal and is only love. There is one thing you can be assured of in all your troubles, battles against sin and temptations: The fatherly heart of God will not give you up for lost. His heart sympathizes with you in love. He wants to help you. He wants to lead you along the right path. He will carry it out!

27

You complain that everything around you is so dead and cold. You are lonely in your family, in your circle of friends, in your church. But that cannot be God's will. God is a Father. He loves you. He wants you to be loved and happy. He is showing you a way. Give others much love, and you will harvest love.

However, if your heart is dead and cold and cannot love, there is a flame which can make even your heart burn. It is the flame of love which burns in the Father's heart and which has flared up mightily in Jesus. Let God's heart enkindle you and you will also become a flame of love. Yes, your love will be like a sun, which shines upon all the cold hearts around you with its goodness and friendliness and sets them on fire with love. Then you will no longer be alone.

You wish that streams of blessing would flow forth from your life. The love of God wants to fulfill your wish. That is why He places an altar in every human life. There He is seeking sacrifices, brought to Him out of love. Only when there are sacrifices upon the altar, can the flame of sacrifice be set ablaze. To the extent that this flame blazes, it will be a flame of God, shining forth brightly, setting others on fire and blessing them.

29

Do you find that you have resigned yourself to the difficulties and sins in your life? Do you think that things cannot be changed? As long as you do, your situation will remain the same. Not until you begin to reckon with God, who still performs miracles today and who always has help prepared, will there be a difference. Praise His omnipotence over the impossible situations in faith, and in prayer take the promises of God and hold them out to Him as an IOU which He has to pay. Then you will experience the miracles of God, His help, transformation in your life and in the hearts and relationships of others.

30

The eyes of God are searching every country for those who keep faith. Through them He can do His great deeds; through them He can glorify Himself. Through men of faith He can manifest His power, His glory and His miracles before men. How the Father must suffer when He sees all the accomplices Satan has to do his work. God the Father has so few children who are filled with zeal to magnify the glory of His name here on earth by believing in Him, by taking risks of faith and walking in the obedience of faith. His eyes are watching to see whether you will commit yourself to ways of faith.

MAY

1

You ask what is the quickest way to escape from this suffering. Such a question should not be your first and foremost concern. The most important thing is to suffer correctly, so that fruit can grow out of it. Then you will not have suffered in vain. Take care that you suffer patiently and that you humble yourself beneath the powerful hand of God. By taking care that you have the proper attitude to your suffering, all false cares will yield and you will be victorious in your suffering. It will bear fruit for eternity.

2

You are right in saying: 'If a war of total annihilation breaks out, it will be darker than ever on earth. The earth will be completely enveloped in night and darkness.' However, when this night reaches its darkest point, the light of God will shine most brightly—for you, for those who are His own. Then we will see the truth of this verse: "Darkness shall cover the earth and thick darkness the peoples; but the Lord will rise upon you, and his glory will be seen upon you." Then you can walk in this light step by step.

Isaiah 60:2

3

Why do we want to make ourselves independent and separate from God? The unconscious motive is often: 'Then I no longer have to follow God's will.' However, if we are not interested in God's will and His commandments in our everyday life, God will not be interested in us during the time of distress. The prodigal son had to suffer bitterly while he was separated from his father during a time of famine. He did not receive any help. And we will not either, unless we return and become prepared to live out the will and commandments of God.

MAY   **4**

Chastenings and blows of God bring about decisions. Some
people become hardened and embittered, when blows of
judgment strike them. Others experience a turning point in
their life which brings them salvation and happiness. What
would you like them to bring you? The outcome rests in
your hand. Choose! Whoever humbles himself beneath the
chastening hand of God will experience transformation, grace
and salvation.

5

Why does God come to the weak and the poor? He feels
sorry for them. They have no other helper besides Him. And
so He sends them help. They have to put their trust in
the strength and greatness of their Father. The poor are
blessed—God always bestows His gifts upon them.

6

You think that the darkest hour of your life has begun.
Then you must realize that your hour to be tested has
arrived. This is the most important, most decisive hour. It
is the hour in which God will test you to see whether you
trust Him in darkest night. Now you only have to say one
sentence to pass this test: 'My Father, I do not understand You, but I trust You!' And great things have been
wrought in you for time and eternity.

7

Childlike trust has power. If it can charm the heart of an
earthly father, how much more will it be able to charm the
heart of God, who is the prototype of all fatherhood and
who is only love. And love is overpowered most quickly
through childlike trust. Practise it!

You are longing to come closer to God, your Father. You want to have a deep personal relationship with Him. You would like to be united with Him. However, you cannot find the way. Why not? You must be avoiding the way which would bring you closer to God. Through the cross we become more tightly bound to God. Whoever embraces His cross lovingly will be united with Jesus and the Father. However, whoever flees the cross, whoever protests against it in his heart, flees from God and will be separated from Him.

9

The Psalmist prays: "Lord, hasten to my aid!" The Spirit of God gave Him this prayer, because God really does hasten to aid us. Like a father, He comes quickly when His child is in need. He hastens to you when you call to Him in your need. But do you really want His help? When we call upon the Father trusting in His aid, we will find the solution for all hardships, worries and difficulties in our life. Therefore, don't brood over your needs. Bring them to God. Cry out to Him, and the answer will soon appear.   *Psalm 22:20*

10

What is awaiting you in the near future? Expect something good. God is good and as a Father He has good things in store for His child. However, God seems to be a hard Lord to those who are evil and mistrusting. In their hearts and lives they erect a barrier against proofs of God's goodness. Therefore, they harvest what they have sown in mistrust. They will be unhappy and remain unhappy, for we receive what we expect from God. So expect good things from Him, and you will experience His great goodness.

God wants to have His children, whom He created, very close to Him, just as a father does. Therefore, He has opened wide the door to His house by paving the way through the suffering and death of His Son. Now the Father is waiting for us to live our lives for Him, for that close relationship day after day. Every new commitment, every loving act of trust, binds us more tightly to the Father.

12

God's mighty creation of giant mountains and wide seas tells us how great God is. But it also shows us how small we are. And still we are impudent enough to dare to oppose the will of God, the will of the almighty Creator and Lord, and to rebel against Him. We have lost the proper sense of relationship towards God. The mighty creation of God wants to teach us this. It is calling us to humble ourselves before such a Lord, to worship Him and to commit our wills to Him. It is the best will, because it is the will of a Father who is nothing but love.

13

You are tormented because you can no longer understand God's actions. However, it has to be that way. If we sinful, created men could always understand God in His thoughts and leadings, He would no longer be God, whose thoughts are higher than our thoughts. We cannot comprehend them. But they are always wonderful; they are always inspired by love. He is leading us in a wonderful manner, according to eternal plans for our best interest. He is leading us to His goal. Desire to be what you are: a creature that can never understand God, but that can trust Him without bounds. Then you will be freed from your tormenting thoughts.

Fear and dread of what lies ahead are trying to devour your soul. Leave behind everything that makes you afraid. Go forward in spirit, and place yourself in the shadow of His wings. Begin to sing for joy, because you have a refuge which the Father has prepared for you in love. There you will be secure during the time of evil. You will be hidden in the hands of the Father, who lovingly cares for you.

15

Let us accept the mighty calling which our Lord Jesus Christ has earned for us: To be sons of God, sons of our Father in heaven. The Father bestows His inheritance upon His sons. He says: "All that is mine is yours." Here on earth He distributes His power and His possessions to His sons. However, when they grow up to the full measure of His image, they will inherit everything in the Father's kingdom.

But, at the moment you are sitting about in rags. You complain about all the things that you do not have, and you are unhappy. It is your own fault that you are so poor. You do not avail yourself of the inheritance which belongs to you. It is your own fault that you are a poor beggar child who is lacking so much. And yet you could be so rich, that you would not be lacking anything, if you would hold out your hands in faith. *Luke 15:31*

16

Do not be so concerned about the approaching troubles. Meditate on God, your Father and the help that He has already prepared for you. Look towards God. Behold, He is coming! He comes when everything seems to be dark and hopeless. He comes to help.

There are eternal and holy laws. Jesus tells us about them. He says that people who follow His call by giving up their rights and privileges, their possessions and things which have become dear to them, are taken care of by the heavenly Father Himself in wonderful and miraculous ways. He wants to share His inheritance with them here on earth. So commit yourself to giving up and forsaking. Then in accordance with the laws of God, you will be richly blessed with gifts.

18

Perhaps you have been put out of circulation through sickness or old age. You keep coming up against blank walls. You want to live and work; you are thirsty for joy. Yet you already seem to be counted among the dead. But the living God, Who awakened Jesus from the dead, wants His creatures and especially His children to be filled with life and joy. Seek this life in Him and not in health and new work. Then you will find lasting, joy-filled life without a shadow. That is why God has brought you out of the life which was filled with human joys and pleasures. He wanted to give you true life. Believe this!

19

Autonomy, dissociation from the Father is sin. It is separation from God, our Father. It is sin against the love of the Father. This sin hurts God; it makes His heart bleed. He calls to us: 'Turn about. Don't make your decisions in a human manner any longer.' Live in dependence upon your heavenly Father alone. He is waiting so much for the sign of your love. He is longing for you, His child. He wants you to live in complete dependence upon Him. He wants you to live in a relationship of intimate love with Him. Do not make Him wait.

You do not know how God will solve your difficulties. God will not tell you in advance. You do not have to know "how". But one thing is certain: God as your Father will solve your difficulties. May this knowledge be enough for you. Praise His love which cannot do otherwise than help you, and you will be comforted.

21

God the Father has a goal for our lives. We are not supposed to be living in vain, but we are supposed to bring forth abundant fruit. So the Father comes to us as the Vine-dresser. Wisely He prunes the vines so that they do not bear any grapes in the first years. The more He prunes them, the more fruit they will bear in the years to come. Jesus has given us this picture for the times when we seem to be bearing no fruit. We seem to be only suffering, just withering away. In these times we should rejoice in the assurance that we are being prepared for greater fruitfulness.

22

It is often the religious who fall into the sin of trying to live their lives separated from God. Basically we are doing what we want to do. Hypocritically we often try to cover up the sin of living our lives separated from the Father.

It is a matter of continually testing to what extent I am really living in childlike dependence upon the Father in every-day matters. We have to ask the Holy Spirit for light in this matter. When we stand on our own two feet and make our own decisions without God, our lives will not bring forth fruit. The more we depend upon God in the smallest matters of life, the more fruit we will have later. Then we will have done everything in God.

The Lord says:

> "Ephraim, how could I part with you?
> Israel, how could I give you up?
> My heart recoils from it,
> my whole being trembles at the thought.
> I will not give rein to my fierce anger.
> I am the Holy One in your midst
> and have no wish to destroy."

It is the heart of God the Father. How can I gain access to this heart? It is closed to the self-righteous, to the high and mighty, to the clever, to the proud. But it is wide open for the humble, the contrite, the penitent sinners. He pours out the abundance of His merciful love upon them. In this way the Father is calling you. He wants to reveal His heart to you so that you can know how wonderful He is.

Hosea 11:8, 9

24

You see the beauty of creation. You see how God created every flower and every small animal in a wonderfully different way. But people are a thousand times more valuable to God. than all the glory of the world of creation. He created them in His image. He calls them His children. He delivered up His Son to death for them. How precious you are in the eyes of God! May this knowledge comfort you when you are tempted. It is true—you are loved!

25

You do not know how you can survive the fears of the dreadful war that is threatening to break out. However, when your fears are about to overwhelm you, the peace and comfort of God will be greater than ever. They will be greater than your fear. Begin to count on it now. You can be sure that you will experience what you believe.

No human being has ever been so hurt and insulted through sin as God. But never has a human being been able to speak so many words of infinite mercy to those who have sinned against him and who have created difficulties for him with their sins as God has. In response to His mercy God has a right to expect that we sinners be merciful to one another. Therefore, be merciful to your neighbour if he hurts you, so that the mercy of God will not be transformed into flaming wrath, which would send you into the eternal damnation like the unmerciful servant.

27

God our Father let His only Son go the way of the Lamb. Like a lamb, Jesus let Himself be dragged to the slaughter-house. "When he was reviled, he did not revile in return; when he suffered, he did not threaten." Now God is seeking the signs of the Lamb in His children. Always choose this way and you will have the authority which you long for. The love of God will give it to you. It has been promised to those who follow Him like lambs. *1 Peter 2:23*

28

You are longing to experience God's love. When will you experience it most strongly? When will His heart of love be opened most widely for you? When you love God. How do you love Him? By wanting what He wants. By agreeing to His thoughts and His plans for you. By placing your trust in Him, even when you do not understand His actions, even when He gives you a cross to bear. His Son carried the cross of the world for you. Follow Him with your own cross, and your love for God will be activated. In response He will let you taste His love for you.

You cannot understand why the verse "affliction is preparing an eternal weight of glory" is not being fulfilled in your life. You are suffering. You are comfortless. None of the beams of the glory of God's love manages to penetrate into your heart. But the Father who is Love knows how you can be comforted. He is saying to you, 'Do not bear your cross like a slave who is forced to bear it. Bear it out of love for Jesus.' Bear it trusting in the Father's love. Bear it committed to His will. Then your cross will begin to shine. You will become happy, and you too will shine in His love.

2 Corinthians 4:17

30

You are in night, in suffering, perplexed and helpless. You do not see the way out. Your Father, who loves you, sees you and your difficulties. He calls to you: 'If you are in night, I want to be in your Light. If you are in suffering, I want to be your Comfort. If you are helpless, I want to be your Helper. If you are perplexed, I want to be your Advisor.' Listen to His voice. Then your heart will become quiet.

31

Since eternity God in His love and tender care has thought of His children who will have to live through the hour of midnight here on earth. In His Word He has already prepared comfort and help for them. He says that all who call upon the name of the Lord will be delivered. Therefore, call upon His name now, and you will be comforted, and on the day of trouble you will experience the fulfillment.

Joel 2:32

God the Father is seeking people who will listen to the lament of His heart, which He has so often expressed: "My people have committed two evils: they have forsaken me, the fountain of living waters..." Or: "When they were fed to the full, they were filled, therefore they forgot me..." Or: "I am weary of bearing them."

The Father's heartache can only be relieved through the love of His children. They express their love for Him when they cry tears of repentance, when they trust Him, when they are willing to be true children, obedient, small and dependent upon Him. God is waiting. Yes, He is continually asking us to love Him. Who can hurt and disappoint this heart of love?

Jeremiah 2:13. Hosea 13:6. Isaiah 1:14

2

God tore His beloved Son from His heart and delivered Him up to rebels and murderers. This sight made the Father's heart bleed. He did it for us, because His love for us is so great. Therefore, He should receive a continual harvest of thanksgiving from His children, a thanksgiving of trust and faith, even when we do not understand Him.

3

God makes us a big offer. He says: 'Ask much, and it will be given you. Heaven and earth are Mine. All of My messengers are at My disposal. They are there to serve ME, to carry out My commands. They are sent forth to serve you —"ten thousand times ten thousand"—a mighty power. What more do you need? So ask for much, ask Me for big things, and I will give them to you.'   *Hebrews 1:14. Daniel 7:10*

You would like to get to know the Father. Our Lord Jesus Christ wants to lead you to Him. But He can only bring you to the Father if you go the same way He went as the Son of God. It is the way of the cross. It was a way of poverty, lowliness, obedience and disgrace. Even today it is the way which leads to the city of God, to the Father's house. Go this way, and you will get to know the Father and His love. He opens His heart to those who go the way of Jesus.

5

You are worrying about how you will get through the desert stretches in your life. How will you be able to cope with loneliness, illness, disagreeable things, impossibilities? But God is not worried when we go through such periods. He says to you: 'If you are in the wilderness, I will prove to you that I am your Father, the same Father who once long ago gave the children of Israel quails and manna when they were hungry. Today also on dark ways I will go before you in a pillar of cloud or a pillar of fire. I will pave your way. With My presence I will bring you comfort and new strength. Is that enough for you?'

6

The heart of the Father is the source of all love. If a person resists our plea for help, we appeal to his heart, to his sympathy, to his compassion. Who can express what God's heart is like! Before it all human love fades into oblivion. Therefore, no one calls upon the divine heart of the Father in vain. It is overflowing with compassion and mercy. So, those who really appeal to the heart of God in the assurance of His love for us have never yet been disappointed.

You wonder why you have to go ways of such suffering. Only paths through the night lead to light. God, who loves you, wants all your ways to end in light, in great joy. Therefore, He has to lead you through night n w

8

Your heart has been wounded by suffering and by the blows of God. Like a child, place yourself in your Father's arms and let Him love you back to health. God never wounds us without healing us and quickening us. He is waiting for His sick child so that He can do something good for him. So come!

9

You are sad. Why? Because you are living in yourself and not in God. It is a matter of living in His presence. You must realize: God is there. You are not alone for a single second. He surrounds you. He sees you. He bears everything with you. He wants to help you. Always live in the assurance that God is present. This consciousness of His presence will transform everything for you, and your sadness will disappear.

10

God wants to live within us. His love is longing to make His dwelling-place in our hearts. However, we must love Him. If we do not, He will not come to us. That is why we must continually ask for love for God and our neighbour, and we must practise it. Love brings God down to us. Could there be anything more wonderful than God making His dwelling place in our hearts?

Say to God, your Father: 'I thank You that I do not have to reckon only with money, gifts and human capabilities, but with Your mighty hand that created the universe. You command, and behold, what was missing is now there.'—And if we claim this with thanksgiving, we will receive all the help we need.

12

The eyes of God are looking for one thing: faith. They are looking to see whether they can find children that can anticipate and sing of the coming morning in the midst of distress and night. Such trust wins over the heart of the Father, and such children will always experience the morning, the rising sun. Therefore, be such a child.

13

You are seeking. What are you seeking? Are you seeking something that would satisfy you and make you happy? Here is an answer: "You will seek me and find me!" Thus says the God who has created you, who knows you and loves you, who wants to give you what you are seeking. And that is love. If you go to Him, He will give you more than any human being could. You are seeking security. He will give it to you; no one else can. You are seeking satisfaction, a person who is completely available for you, who could be your intimate friend. The One who does not lie, who cannot disappoint us tells you: "I want to give you life abundantly." So turn to Him. He loves you. He will answer you and fulfil the longings of your heart. He cannot and will not disappoint you.   *Jeremiah 29:13. John 10:10*

You cannot understand that God, who calls Himself a Father, can impose such a difficult cross upon you? You have probably forgotten that each of us is a sinner. Sinners need to have crosses and sufferings in their lives so that they can be chastised, purified and transfigured. Otherwise, they would never reach the goal of the glory of God. For without sanctification no one will see the Lord.

Perhaps it is not difficult for you to believe that God the Father will help you with your personal problems and carry you through. However, you are worried, because you do not know what it will be like when times of affliction descend upon all of us. But you can be sure that His help will be in proportion to the amount of destruction. Hours of need, of terror and destruction were always special hours of God, when He proved His glorious might. Consider this verse: "Nothing can hinder the Lord from saving by many or by few." 1 Samuel 14:6

Whenever we have to experience how incapable and untalented we are, the moment has arrived for us to call down the love of the Father. At such moments His love will come to us as never before. If we would only believe this: These are the moments when we entice the Father to have mercy upon us and to show us His miraculous power, His help and His beneficence. He will shower us with His love. Let us take advantage of these moments. They are opportunities to experience the love and aid of the Father more than ever.

"The Father himself loves you." Jesus says this—Jesus who is Truth and who knows the Father intimately. Therefore, believe that you are loved by God the Father. Tell yourself this over and over again: 'I am loved!' Then you will experience that trust in the love of the Father heals all the sickness of your soul. *John 16:27*

18

God has a heart full of love. That is why He consoles us like little children by saying: "If you are at the ends of the earth and at the abyss of death—behold, I am there also. I am with you to help you, to protect you and to sustain you." So answer Him: 'Yes, Lord, You are everything—and whoever has You, has everything that he needs, even in death.'

19

Perhaps you are saying: 'I have received so little from the hand of God. He has fulfilled so few of my wishes.' Whose fault is it that your life is so poor? Certainly not God's! Let God ask you a few questions: 'Have you fulfilled My wishes and My will by living according to My commandments? Have you put Me in first place in your life and loved Me above all? Have you loved your fellow men with a love that bears all, endures all and does not become bitter? Have you honoured your parents? Have you slandered anyone, lied, stolen or committed adultery?'

There is a verse in the Scriptures which tells us who will receive good things from God. It is: "We have confidence before God and we receive from Him whatever we ask, because we keep his commandments and do what pleases him." So act according to the will of God and you will experience the truth of these words: "I will rejoice in doing them good." *1 John 3:21b, 22. Jeremiah 32:41*

Who continues to be a slave to the law although he believes in Jesus? Only those who refuse to be remoulded into true children who have a trusting love. To be sure, a child of the Father follows the Son as a disciple of the cross and is prepared to lose his life and to forsake those things which are precious to him. However, he can also rejoice over the presents of the Father and over His creation. He can rejoice over people and things which God gives us as a greeting of His fatherly love. And he can love them without becoming attached to them. To live as true children of the Father, free from the law and bound through love to the way of Jesus makes us happy and opens the door for many others to come to the Father's house.

21

Those who love us are glad when they see us joyful and they do everything they can to make us happy. But no one loves us as much as God does. Should it not be His greatest desire to see us, His children, happy? Let us believe this, and believing, let us be happy like little children. When we expect good things from our Father, we will make Him happy. Let us not grieve His loving heart by mistrusting Him.

22

God loves us. That is why He trains us and chastens us as a true Father. He stops showering us with His gifts if we use them selfishly or disobediently. Jesus wants us to experience the kingdom of heaven and to discover how kind He is. Therefore, He keeps caling to us: 'Repent!' For the heart of the Father is wide open for all who are sorry for their sins and who turn over a new leaf. Then He can shower us with His goodness.

Your heart is filled with anxiety. Peace has departed from you. You have been gripped with fear of the coming apocalyptic times. God, your Father, wants to help you. He says: "O that you had hearkened to my commandments! Then your peace would have been like a river." He is showing you the way. Now it is a matter of accepting the commandments of God as binding and doing His will day by day. Then you will be at one with God and you will be strong and Your heart will be filled with peace. In times of great tribulation this peace will not depart from you; it will be like a river which flows out of your union with the will of God.   *Isaiah 48:18*

24

What is the greatest gift that God can grant us? Himself, His inherent nature, which is "love". He does not want to keep this love for Himself. He wants it to be our portion also. That is why He sent Jesus, love manifest in the flesh, who brought this love to earth to redeem us to love. Let us draw love from His fountain of grace, and then we will have the greatest present, the greatest happiness for time and eternity—love. Nothing can make us so happy as loving.

25

Look at the fatherly hands of God. Look at the way they work in sinful men. These fatherly hands place the robe of righteousness and the most precious ring of divine love on those who approach the Father like the Prodigal Son and say, "Father, I have sinned against heaven and before you." Place yourself in these fatherly hands when your mistakes and your sins make you sorrowful and they will soothe you and be kinder to you than you can imagine.   *Luke 15:21-22*

God needs people who are persistent in prayer like the Syrophoenician woman who refused to be turned away. He is waiting for people, who when they at first seem to receive a stone instead of bread, nevertheless persevere and hold God by His word: "What man of you, if his son asks him for a loaf, will give him a stone?" There is no such father—or he wouldn't be a true father. 'Therefore, You can never give me a stone when I ask You for something!' Say this to the heavenly Father. In answer to such a humble prayer God will turn the stone—even if you are already holding it in your hands—into a loaf of bread. He keeps His word, when we believe Him.   *Matthew 7:9*

27

Perhaps you are complaining that God, who is Love, has laid a cross upon your shoulders that is especially heavy. Your heavenly Father answers you: Your cross is not heavier than you can bear. Yes, if your cross is heavy, then the blessing it will bring is also heavy. When I give you a heavy cross, you must see that I love you. It is a gift for my favourite children; I intend to give them special blessings. Your cross is a treasure. Pick it up, trusting that I have hidden a rich blessing in it.

28

Can we ever measure the fatherly goodness of God? He always has to bestow good things upon us. He is intent on making His children happy. Now His children should sing songs of praise to Him. By proclaiming how good the Father is and by thanking Him for it, we open His hands; and the blessings, grace and the presents of His fatherly goodness will stream down upon us. So give thanks more often and you will receive more, yes, you will receive abundantly.

We say: 'It is difficult to believe in the love of God.' But God has proved that He loves us. Out of love for us He underwent unspeakable suffering by delivering His Son into the hands of men, and suffering with Him when He was tormented and ill-treated until He was no longer recognizable and then finally killed. The actions of God are always love, even when we do not understand them. It is at these times that we should love Him most—for the sake of His great work of love, the sacrifice of Jesus Christ. We should honour Him by trusting Him.

30

The way God is leading you has been planned and thought out for you in His heart since eternity. It is *your* way. It is the best way for you and will bring you to a glorious goal. The Father is waiting for you to accept your way from His hand as His child. He is waiting for you to go this way with your whole heart. So speak: 'Thank You, my Father for leading me the best way.' Thanksgiving will open your eyes so that you can see the blessings of God which lie upon this way.

JULY 1

You have lost courage. You are on the verge of despair. Your sin seems to be binding you with chains; you seem to be a prisoner. But God your Father loves you. He has given you a door which leads out of your dark dungeon. This door is repentance. The penitent sinner is given forgiveness through the blood of Jesus. And forgiveness makes everything new, you and your whole life. Such creative power lies in repentance that it can even work retroactively and renew what had been destroyed.

God has opened the door to the Father's house through Jesus Christ. Yet so often we live outside this house; we have made so few discoveries about living in the Father's house. In the Father's house the child is surrounded by joy and security. There the child is at home. There he is surrounded by love and can bring everything to the Father. He receives more counsel and help than he could ask or imagine. He is completely committed to the will of the Father and to His leadings. His deepest need is solved when he receives fatherly forgiveness. Jesus wants to draw us into the Father's house, when He tells us we should become like little children without rights, demands, privileges, respect, influence, importance and ability to make our decisions. Who will follow Jesus to the Father's house?

3

In order to attain important things in our life we have often risked a great deal. Now God as our Father is asking us to take another risk. God is waiting for people who are willing to step into uncertainty, because they believe that He is capable of doing everything He promises. Such people will experience the deeds and miracles of God today. With their God they will "leap the rampart".   *Psalm 18:29*

4

God the Father has shown us His greatest love by delivering up His only Son to torment and death on the cross according to His own free will and decision. And Jesus has shown us His greatest love by taking up His cross voluntarily out of love for us. Now God is waiting for us to take up our cross and to bear it out of love for Him. Then we shall be transformed into the image of Jesus.

The Father of love is very, very sad when His admonitions and His work of purification have no effect upon us. This always happens when we protest against the chastisements of God and hit His chastening hand. The sorrow that we cause the Father when we do this cannot be expressed in words—we are destroying the work that He wants to accomplish in us. So it is usually we ourselves who are guilty when we are not transformed into the image of Jesus as He wants us to be. It is usually our own fault when the Lord has to think up new ways of chastisement for us in order to set us straight. Whoever humbles himself before God can escape many chastisements.

6

God is a Father of love. It is the nature of love to care for the other. So let your Father take care of all the things that befall you and oppress you. Do not worry and make plans in advance. As a child you cannot do it right anyway. Leave all the planning and preparation to the Father. He is all-wise, all-powerful, all-knowing. He only expects one thing from you—that you care for your small daily portion. However, leave the further developments to God's planning. He is wonderful in counsel and excellent in wisdom.

7

You would like to show God your love, but you do not know how. Give Him your will. That means giving Him everything. Only choose what He desires. Choose His way, the way He wants to lead you. Choose to have what He gives you. Choose to do without that which He witholds from you or which He takes from you. Give Him all your own wishes and desires. Then you will have proved that you love God above all. God will answer your love by coming to you and making His home with you. *John 14:23*

"My Father is greater than all." What a pledge! His love is greater than all human love and all human willingness to help. The help which He can offer is greater than your difficulty. His forgiveness is greater than your burden of sin. If the Father is greater than all, then He is also greater than the anguish which the approaching times of tribulation may bring. Therefore, in every difficulty say, 'Father, You are greater than all.' And you will experience this truth.

John 10:29

9

When a child is fearful, his mother takes him in her arms and keeps him from seeing what makes him afraid. The Father in heaven will do the same thing for us. In times of tribulation He will hide us in His shelter. He will close our eyes and take us into His arms so that we scarcely see anything of the horror. We will sense only one thing: We are secure and surrounded by love. We are protected from the tribulation. We are sheltered from it by His protecting presence. He will sustain us.

10

We often have knowledge of God but no longer any living relationship to Him. Often God stands outside our daily life. God is no longer relevant to our daily life. If this is a picture of your spiritual life, it is time to turn over a new leaf. It could be that the same thing will happen to you that happened to the rich farmer who worked and lived apart from God and took his own precautions for the future. Perhaps God will say to you also: "This night your soul is required of you." How will you be able to stand, if you are not rich in God?"

Luke 12:20

Even on the most unpleasant days do not forget to say, 'I thank You, my Father.' Especially on such days it is a great help to list all the blessings that the Lord has given you for body and soul. Giving thanks will make the overcast day bright. God sends you dark days only to test you, to see whether you will remain faithful in giving Him the thanks that you owe Him. Whoever cannot give thanks on cloudy days has not yet learned his lesson. Only sacrifice of thanksgiving—for it is a sacrifice to give thanks when you feel down—is precious to God and carries weight.

12

When a little boy has a big, strong man at his side who will stand up for him, he will be helped. Often we are so small, weak and helpless in the face of our needs, difficulties and tasks. However, the Lord who has made heaven and earth assures us that He wants to stand up for us. That is why His words "Be of good courage!" are not empty words. What can we possibly be missing when the Lord of lords assures us: "I, the Lord, shall create!"   *Isaiah 45:8*

13

There is very little accomplished in the busy affairs of everyday life that brings blessing. Everything that is important and of eternal importance grows out of time apart with God. Therefore, seek to have more quiet time alone with God. There is nothing that can be substituted for abiding in the presence of God. The greater the load of work and the more difficulties there are, the more time you should be spending alone with God. Through prayer you will become strong for times of temptation. Only when you have quiet time, will you be able to bear your work load properly. Seek the presence of God. In His presence everything will be solved that you cannot solve by yourself.

God is the true Father of all who bear the name of children. What could make Him more happy than a person who is really a child in relationship to Him, who comes to Him in complete trust and who expects gifts of love from Him? From millions of people the Father receives only mistrust, and that hurts His heart. Would you like to be the one who makes Him happy? Trust in His love; trust Him completely.

Ephesians 3:15

15

In the Word of God you have the pledge of the fatherly love of God: He wants to care for you! So when mountains of cares and worries begin to arise before your eyes, say over and over again: 'The Father cares! The Father cares!' Yes, the Father will take care of everything as only perfect Love can. This love has thought out everything for you in divine omnipotence and wisdom. Let this knowledge be turned into praise. When you thank Him for taking care, your heart will be filled with comfort and peace.

16

If God is our Father, He has the right to rejoice over His children, to rejoice because they reflect something of His divine nature. He is longing to find His traits in them. Whoever surrenders willingly to His chastisements and believes in the redemption of Jesus, will bring Him this joy. He will be transformed into the image of His Son. Let us not keep the Father waiting so long before He can see His reflection in us; let us strive to make God happy by letting Him see this picture. Let us "strive for holiness".

Hebrews 12:14

God our Father is longing for us to be completely dependent upon Him. Why? Because He who loves us is yearning for us to return His love. Becoming dependent upon Him of our own free will is a sign that we love Him in return. It is a sign of trust. God shows His love to those who are prepared to be dependent upon Him. They will experience the abundance of His love.

18

Perhaps you are at your wits' end. You don't know how you are going to manage with your poor health, with your lack of strength, with your problems at work. But believe that it is good when you reach the end of your tether. Then Someone else can make a new beginning. There is a verse that is valid and will take effect when you claim it: "Behold, I make all things new."

Yes, God the Lord, who loves you, says: 'I make all things new, even yourself! But you must bring Me your old life, including everything that is called sin. A new house can only be built when the old, dilapidated house has been demolished. Then I will blot out your sins through the blood of Jesus and forgive you.' So come with your sins; confess them to someone. Then you will be happy that you were at the end of your tether. That will be the turning point of your life, the new beginning.   *Revelation 21:5*

19

Fear of the coming times just about wrings your heart. You think you can no longer be happy. But then the voice of Someone comes to you, who alone knows God from the beginning of time. It is the voice of Jesus calling to us, "Have faith in God."—"And will not God vindicate his elect, who cry to him day and night? I tell you he will vindicate them."

Mark 11:22. Luke 18:7, 8

You are happy that God in His goodness has given you so much here on earth, things that you love and that make your life rich. Perhaps they are close friends or your family; perhaps it is your profession, your talents, your possessions, house and garden. But have you ever considered the fact that if God has given you so much out of love, you have so many good things to give others? Give them to Him who is worthy of all presents from us. Do not keep Him waiting for your presents. He is waiting for you to return His love.

21

Your cross is weighing heavily upon you. You can no longer believe in the love of God. You say that you believe in Jesus Christ, so you must also believe in the heavenly Father. You confess that God is a Father and a Father of love. Therefore, you must admit that everything the Father does, He does out of love, even when He chastises you by giving you a cross. That is exactly when He is working on you so that He can transfigure you for heavenly glory. Your cross which is now weighing heavily upon you will transfigure you and lift you up to heaven. Therefore, love your cross. God has given it to you as a key that will open the door to heaven one day. Do not lose it. It is very precious.

22

We often think we are alone and forgotten. But that is a false assumption: The eyes of the Father never lose sight of us. He is looking into our heart. He perceives every emotion and every thought, every temptation and every sorrow. He is looking after us in infinitely merciful love. He is waiting for us. He is waiting for us to catch His glance and to be led by His eyes, to let ourselves be comforted, helped and set on the right path through His love. So look to Him, and let Him help you. Give Him the response of your love.

God is the Almighty and is also our loving Father. He would like our lives to be filled with signs of His wonders and grace to the glory of His name. However, this can only happen in so far as we are willing to dare to go ways of faith and take risks of faith. According to the measure of our faith we will experience the miracles and signs of God and glorify Him.

24

You think that you are delivered up to the forces of evil which your sin has set in action. If that were so, God would no longer be alive—God, who out of love sacrificed His Son so that we might be saved. He is showing us a way to escape from this evil: We can repent of our sin. Repentance can make sin our gain. In His goodness God gives us sinners additional gifts of grace: thanksgiving for forgiveness, love for Jesus, the Redeemer, hatred against sin, humility, faith in the blood of Jesus, that cleanses us from all sins. Who can comprehend God's merciful love towards sinners? So let us entrust ourselves to this love.

25

You no longer see any help in your difficult situation, no help in the face of the threatening destruction that will bring terror to the whole earth. Trust God! It is written, "I will deliver him." Cling to this verse. Do not give up in despair or let it have any room in your heart, for the Lord says: "Woe unto him that is faint-hearted! for he believeth not; therefore shall he not be defended." However, those who fear Him, trust Him and expect the best from Him will experience grace and comfort—today as well as long ago.

Psalm 91:14. Ecclesiasticus 2:13

If God loves us like a Father, He has to train us and chasten us like children. But it hurts Him to chasten us. Because He is love, it is difficult for Him to strike us. Believe in His love! Over and over again He has to have mercy upon His child. He has to comfort him, to refresh him and to make him happy. In the midst of His anger He is calling to us: "Is Ephraim my dear son? Therefore my heart yearns for him; I will surely have mercy upon him." Cling to this promise.   *Jeremiah 31:20*

27

God is a Father. He comforts us with respect to the difficulties which will come upon us—He assures us that He knows those who trust in Him, and He will not confound them. We have no reason to mistrust such a God who would deliver up His Son Jesus Christ to such tremendous suffering for our sake. He has proved that "the Lord is good". And because He is the same yesterday and today He will prove it also in times of great need. He will espouse and help us.
Nahum 1:7

28

You believe in Jesus and are a child of God the Father. Still you assert that you are not happy. There is a reason. You are looking for happiness in the wrong place. Deep joy lies hidden in the cross. If you want to taste it, take a different attitude towards your cross. Accept it as a greeting from the Father, as a bearer of blessings. And expect that the cross will bring you the happiness you long for. Then you will experience in truth: Crying turns to laughter. The cross brings joy!

The fact that God sends us suffering and crosses which cost us tears seems to be incompatible with the love of God which counts our tears. The Lord replies: "Blessed are those who mourn." The blessing is hidden in the love of the cross. Are you lacking this love for your cross? If so, you cannot be happy. Love your cross as a gift from the Father and your love will make the things that are difficult for you disappear. The secret of the love of the Father and the love of Jesus will be revealed to you and will make you happy—even in tears. *Psalm 56:9. Matthew 5:4*

30

God is yearning for people who behave like children towards Him and are dependent upon Him. As a Father, God would like to intervene and care for His children. However, if we seek to manage the problems in our daily life all by ourselves, we will not experience His care and intervention. We will deprive ourselves of the most precious thing in our life: Having a carefree, happy heart. So let go of your self-will, which seeks to manage your problems all by itself, and God will help you.

31

Who are the people that experience the tender, loving care of God the most? Those who tread the way of the cross in the discipleship of our Lord Jesus—those who take up their cross patiently and humbly, expecting all their help to come from God. God sees the image of His Son in them. That moves His heart deeply and entices Him to do good things for them, to refresh them and to comfort them.

Do not pass your happiness by. Someone is offering it to you: a life filled with joy and happiness, authority and love. He who is offering it, guarantees that His offer will never disappoint you. It is the Lord, your God. He keeps His promises. In the twinkling of an eye, you can become a richer and happier person. Reach out! However, when you open your hand, you must throw away the things that you are holding on to. They are usually things which will not make you happy and which are not even good. Throw them away! Place them beneath the cross of Jesus! God the Father has erected this cross out of love—the cross on which His Son hung so that men might find their happiness and bliss there. Only there can you find them. Come to the cross daily with your sins and burdens. There they will be taken away from you, and God will make your life rich and happy. Come to Jesus. He will fulfil the deepest longings of your heart.

2

Who will experience the abundant love, the tender care and the miracles of God the Father? Those who have the courage to become poor in one area or another and expect God to provide for all their needs. God uses the poor to reveal to us how rich He is and how lovingly He cares for His children. Should that not make us want to follow his call to lose our lives and to give up our possessions?

3

You have to go through a desert period in your life. Darkness and desolation seem to be around you. However, with God, who is Love, there are no deserts without oases. You can be sure they are waiting for you. In joyful expectation go forward to find them.

God answers prayers. His Word tells us that. You doubt that
sometimes. Yes, God answers prayers, even if He answers
differently than we had thought. God is a Father and He
does not give His children anything that would be bad for
their body, soul or spirit. He alone with His great wisdom
actually knows what is good for His child and gives him
what he really needs. Therefore, God really did answer your
prayer. He gave you what you ultimately desired, even
though He may not have fulfilled your request. If the Father
had to withhold something from you for your own good, you
can be sure that His loving heart will give you even more
than you asked for, but perhaps in a different way. Open
your eyes, and you will see it.   *Psalm 91:15*

5

Do you feel weak and incapable? If so, rejoice in the assurance of your Father that His grace is sufficient for you. In His
grace is everything that you need. The strength of God and
His grace is manifested in fullness in the weak—this is what
is promised you. Therefore, you are rich when you are poor
in the way of capabilities and talents—yes, even when in faith
in His grace you can boast, with the Apostle Paul, of your
poverty.

6

When a child prays to God the Father, his prayer is powerful
and promising, for God loves children. He listens to the little
ones when they cry and He helps them. However, born-again
children of God are often in danger of losing their childhood
which they have received through Jesus Christ. Childhood
must be practised in life, tested and strengthened by childlike dependence upon the Father, by readiness to be humbled
and by surrender to His will. The earnestness of our dedication will determine how much power our prayers will have.

You see the path mankind has taken. You see that this path of sin may lead to nuclear war and complete destruction. But your Father, who loves you, calls to you: "He is a shield to those who walk in integrity, guarding the paths of justice and preserving the way of his saints." He will make a path in the mighty waters for the godly and the chosen. He will lead them through fire, for they are precious in His sight and He has respect unto His chosen. Take care that you really belong to His chosen.

Prov. 2:7b, 8. Wisdom of Solomon 4:15

8

What are the contents of your prayers? There is a certain prayer which will please the Father and which He will certainly answer. It is the prayer for repentance. Never forget to ask for it. Repentance is blessed, because it drives us into the arms of God, to His very heart. When repentance has found room in your heart, a stream of joy will flow forth. Out of repentance comes new, divine life. Then you will have the love which makes you happy. The heavenly Father wants to give you this gift of repentance. He cannot bear to see anyone remain comfortless.

9

You wonder: 'Why does God who says that He is a Father of love lay this cross upon me?' Do not look at yourself. Look at Jesus, who entered glory through the cross. Your cross is also supposed to be the ship which will bring you to the city of God, which is your destination. Up to this day there is no other way but the way of the cross that leads to glory. It is the cross that brings glory, according to Scripture. Therefore, look forward to the glory. Live now in the faith that you will reach the destination and the difficult things will become easy.

Perhaps you are carrying a heavy burden. It seems to be as big as a mountain. You have not the faintest idea how this mountain will ever be moved. But God in His love has already thought up a way which will help you. Dig underground tunnels in this mountain, burrow your way through bit by bit. Finally the mountain will be undermined. And it will collapse. What are these underground tunnels? They are nothing but small steps of faith. They bring victory and in the place of the mountain, which has collapsed, your life will rise as a new and marvellous work of God.

11

It has become dark upon the earth and darkness is creeping into your heart. However, God is coming to look after His child whenever he is surrounded by darkness and fear. He says to His child: "Fear not, I will help you!" "The sun shall be no more your light by day, but the Lord will be your everlasting light." His light shines more brightly, and His joy is greater than your greatest sadness. May you have that assurance deep in your heart during dark times.

Isaiah 41:13. Isaiah 60:19

12

Do not despise the "meagre" days that do not seem to contain anything special. Do not despise the "small" opportunities, the insufficient energy. God loves the small and lowly—the little town of Bethlehem, the small nation, the "worm Jacob". He is calling to you: "The least one shall become a clan, and the smallest one a mighty nation." That is a law in the kingdom of God. Whoever goes through the meagre days humbly and faithfully will be appointed by the Lord to govern much. He will experience great wonders in God's kingdom. *Isaiah 41:14. Isaiah 60:22*

There is no love that is so bitterly rewarded and so disappointed as the love of the heavenly Father. There is no love that has found so little response. No father has ever loved so much and taken such great pains to instruct and discipline his children as the Father in heaven, and no such love has ever met with such protest and spite as the heavenly Father's love. That is why there is no heart that ought to be filled with such joy as this fatherly heart. May that be the purpose of our life. That would make our lives worth living.

14

We should not let a single day pass without asking God to teach us how to trust in His fatherly love. There is nothing we need more than this trust. Whoever can trust the Father like a child will receive help in all his difficulties. The gift of trust is the most precious gift. And the Father will give it to those who ask for it.

15

Great and powerful is God's love for us. He revealed Himself to us, spoke with us and made His will known to us. He tells us what we should do, what is good for us. Nothing hurts Him more than our ignoring what He says and what He tells us to do. Whoever loves God takes His commandments seriously and seeks to follow them. He will experience that doing the will of God brings him happiness and salvation. This will come forth from a heart which is only love and which has only good intentions for us.

16

God as the Father of love will not let the sky above us become dark without placing any lights of promise on it. Look up to them. They will lighten even your darkness.

You say: 'The die has already been cast. What I hoped for, what I had put all my efforts into has not been successful.' But even if things do seem to be in a mess, they can be changed. Call to God in your distress! His love has good advice and can show you how the situation caused by your mistake can be remedied. It can be restored by calling upon the victorious name of Jesus. Call upon this name and the victory of Jesus will even be able to change things that have already happened.

18

You can sense your spiritual death. Perhaps you have been asking God for a long time to give you new spiritual life. But be assured that because God is love, He wants to give you good things, especially such spiritual life. He is only waiting for you to take the path which leads to new life. Life lies in sacrificing. Only to the extent that you sacrifice will you be alive. So begin to give God something. Sacrifice your time, your money, people or things which you are attached to. And behold, you will come alive and be filled with the joy that God wants to give you.

19

God is Love. Whoever loves has to be with those whom he loves, especially when they are in trouble. The Bible tells us about God, who is eternal Love: "The Lord is round about his people, from this time forth and for evermore." He is there when the need is greatest, when the torches of the most terrible war are hurled. Then He will surround us like mountains that protect us from the terrible things that are approaching from all sides. He, the Almighty, can do such things.   *Psalm 125:2*

It hurts God the Father when we exclude Him from our lives, although we call ourselves His children. We try to do everything with our own strength, capabilities and talents. We think we have to take care of our own security. But when we do that, we lose the most important thing. We lose the close relationship to our heavenly Father and His heart—the daily proofs of His personal love and help. So we stay poor, because we have to do without the proofs of His love and His divine help which alone could help us in many situations.

21

If a child is hurt or if he has a problem, he expects his father to pick him up and comfort him. How much more should we be able to reckon with the love of our heavenly Father in such situations, for His love is a thousand times greater than the love of all earthly fathers. Jesus said: "Come to me, all who labour and are heavy-laden, and I will give you rest!" His words reveal something of the Father's love. Let us come and experience the wonderful rest He gives.

Matthew 11:28

22

You think that when the destruction breaks out you will be surrendered to it just like the others. But God's word tells you differently. It says: "When the righteous cry for help, the Lord hears, and delivers them out of all their troubles ... He keeps all their bones; not one of them is broken." So just take care that you belong to the "righteous", who are made righteous through the blood of Jesus and live according to the commandments of God. Then God's promises of special help and protection will belong to you.

Psalm 34:18, 21

You say: 'I have no talents, no capabilities and no energy. I cannot do anything; I am good for nothing.' The Lord says: 'Then the time has arrived for Me to act. I do not share My power with any human power. But I prove My power through those who cannot do anything by themselves.' So boast of your weakness, and the power of God will take effect in you.

24

Whoever lives like a child completely dependent upon God will experience that God, as a Father, leads him along His wonderful ways. God solves all his difficulties and problems, takes his side in all matters and cares for him. It pays to leave behind all security and to seek only the Kingdom of God, His righteousness, His pleasure. Those who do this will have all else added unto them.

25

Jesus calls to us whenever fear and anguish are about to overpower our hearts: "Believe in God, believe also in me." Believe in the power of God whose presence can transform hell into heaven. Then you will be able to experience a bit of heaven in the midst of hell's onslaught. Stephen experienced this and many others after him. We too will experience the same things, if we believe in the love of God.

John 14:1

26

When you are treading dark trails through the wilderness, live in the assurance that the love of God always has an end to your suffering. Be assured that after dark times the sun will laugh upon you again—and light will begin to shine in on your present darkness.

God seldom gives His children a long-range view of their way. Usually He only lets them see the next stretch that they have to pass through. Why? Because that is the best way to practise faith for the ways that lie in darkness. Since God loves us, He wants to hand us the crown of faith one day. That is why He has to give us such opportunities to practise faith.

28

Times of distress reveal to us what our relationship to the Father is like, whether we have set our hope in men and conditions or whether we have really trusted in God. In such times of need, when we have to suffer for what we had not learned before, God is calling us again to come home into the Father's house. Perhaps it is God's last offer of grace.

So it is a very special and decisive moment when we have firmly reached the end of our confidence in man and earthly conditions. Then a door opens for us. It is a gate of repentance. Whoever repents of these ways of independence and says: 'I have sinned; I have separated myself from God!', will see the doors of the Father's house open, and the love, the tender care and the help of the Father will be his.

29

God is denying you the fulfilment of your fondest dreams. You are tormenting yourself, because you cannot put an end to your craving. But there is a way to help. Say: 'My Father, what You deny me I do not want to have. I only want to have what You have assigned to me. 'There is power in such dedication of the will. It will make your agonizing craving yield. For a heart that rests in the will of God is filled with peace and comfort.

Every time something happens to you or you experience something, listen to this statement: "It is the Lord." Then you will no longer become agitated or annoyed about what happens to you or what people do to you. Now you will be able to see God at work in everything. Humble yourself beneath the hand of God in the knowledge that His heart of love only intends to do good things to you, and His hand will carry out everything for the best. Believe this. Then much of the distress and temptation in your life will no longer be of any importance. Then you will overcome your temptations.

31

You think the way God is leading you is more than you can take. That cannot be. God as a Father does not give His child more burdens than he can carry. If the way is especially hard for you, His love has also thought out special blessing and help. So go the way to the end. At the goal great and wonderful things are awaiting you. Do not look at the way; look at the goal. The way is short and transient. But you will remain at the glorious goal through all eternity.

SEPTEMBER

1

Do we have any idea how much the Father in heaven must suffer when we who were created according to His image often look so unredeemed and deformed? God would not have sacrificed His only Son on the cross if He were not so interested in transforming us into His image, into the image of the glory of God. How interested are you in shining forth the image of God as the redeemed of Jesus? Whoever loves God strives for sanctification, because he wants to fulfil the Father's deepest wish. And whoever strives for sanctification will achieve it, because Jesus has redeemed us to be sanctified.

You are in great distress, because you cannot sense the presence of God and your relationship to Him seems to be dead. Why does God seem to be so strange to you, so far away? You are beginning to doubt His love. But believe that He is showing you His special love now. He wants to make your love pure and true. That is why He is testing it.

Love that stood the test is precious and it will bring you a rich reward. This love proves itself by continuing to trust God even in the midst of temptation and inner conflict, by going His way in obedience and by offering sacrifices. There is no sacrifice which is so great as that which is offered in times of spiritual dryness without feeling anything. Such love is the greatest present you can give the Father.

3

Your heart is depressed when you think about everything that will come to pass. Look up to the hills whence cometh your help, for help will come. It comes from the God who has made heaven and earth and who is the strength of His chosen. By looking away from everything that is threatening the earth and looking up to Him, to whom all power has been given and who can help us in every situation, our heart is transformed. This will make us strong and confident and make fear and doubt yield.

4

Love is generous. God, who is Love, gives an overflowing measure of all that is good. What can prevent Him from doing that? Only we ourselves. Jesus says: "Give, and it will be given to you." But so often we cling to what we have and do not help others who are in need and dilemma. Then God, the Father, has to withhold His gifts from us, because He loves us. He withholds them in order to set us straight again.   *Luke 6:38*

You get scared whenever you think of the coming times. But even in the midst of your fear there is a council before God's throne. His angels are being sent out to guard you on all your ways and even to bear you up on their hands, and to sustain you in all tribulation. Never forget that!

Psalm 91:11, 12

6

Whoever as a child wants to ask and receive much of the Father, must also act like a true child and obey His commandments. Whoever does not do that, whoever e.g. judges, when Jesus tells us expressly not to judge, will be struck by this verse: "Judge not, that you be not judged." God, however, may sometimes punish us by not opening His hand and answering our prayers.   *Matthew 7:1*

7

When you are faced by fears, needs and distress, say again and again: "Thou art my hiding place; thou shalt preserve me from trouble; thou shalt compass me about with songs of deliverance." Then you will experience that words of trust, spoken in the presence of the Father, have power to drive away the enemy who wants to bring us into fear and despair.   *Psalm 32:7*

8

God wants to help His children. However, so often they make themselves independent. They take precautions and make plans by themselves—separated from God. How can He then intervene in their problems and troubles with His help? If we take everything into our own hands, we bind God's hands. Is it any wonder then that our needs are not solved?

Do we protest and rebel against the will of God when suffering hits us? If so, our relationship to God is like that of a servant, who is indignant when he does not receive what he thinks are his rights. But servants are not children. They are excluded from the inheritance. Therefore, turn from the behaviour of a servant. It makes you unhappy and is not pleasing to God. It will keep you from your inheritance. But you have been called to be a child through the sacrificial death of Jesus.

10

It hurts God, the Father, when He has to punish people and nations. However, He has to do it, because we so often do not listen to His admonitions and actually do not want to be freed of our sins. If we could only see the fatherly sorrow of God, we would recognize that we ourselves are often the cause of these blows of judgment. And we are the ones who are in the position of putting an end to the judgments of God through repentance. If you are under such judgment now, God, the Father, is calling to you: 'Repent! Turn from your old ways!' When we have a repentant heart, God in His love will turn judgment into grace.

11

God's way is too difficult for you. You keep asking 'why?' and you do not find any answer. But you would find it, if you came to God your Father and said: 'You alone are wise. Your way is always right. You, God, love me. You alone know what is really best for me and You do the best for me.' If you pray this, you are admitting that God is right and in doing so give honour to Him. Wherever God is honoured, Satan with his temptations has to yield.

You are seeking the solution to a problem that seems to you to be complicated and impenetrable. Do not seek a premature solution to your problems; do not seek to know the outcome of your way. Then your cares and worries will be your own fault. In obedience take the next step on the path which lies before you. God will always show you the next stretch and will pave it for you. If you do that, things will develop further and the will of God will be revealed to you. Leave the final solution to God. He is Love, Therefore, the solution will always be good and will bring the complete answer to questions which are depressing you now.

13

An earthly father who has great influence and power enjoys using these possibilities to help his children, to make their ways straight. How much more then does the heavenly Father enjoy doing such things! Through His wondrous might He wants to pave the way for us. He wants to remove obstacles and make crooked places straight. He enjoys helping us. Yet, He finds so few people who believe it. That is why there are only a few who really experience it!

14

God is saying NO to your way. He is putting up barricades. What should you do? You should say NO to this way also. Trusting your heavenly Father, say: 'I do not want to choose a way which you are preventing me from going. I want to love the way that you have prepared for me. I know that it is the best one, for You have thought it out for me with Your loving heart.' Then your troubles will cease, and you will truly experience that God is leading you on the best way.

God sends you a cross, because as a Father He has to discipline and prepare you. Now He is waiting for your response. Will you respond to the Father like a child? Will He hear you say: 'I want my cross. It comes from Your hands. You gave it to me, and if You do not want to take it away, I will accept it. It is a greeting from You'? Believe that this declaration of will has power in the invisible world. Satan, who hates the cross, will flee from you and Jesus, who humbly carried the cross, will come to you and filled with joy will take you into His arms. In you He has found a true disciple, who has obeyed His command: "If any man would come after me, let him ... take up his cross and follow me." You have refreshed the heart of Jesus and the Father.

Matthew 16:24

16

You say that God has taken away the person who was most precious to you. Your whole happiness centred around him. You cannot live without this person. However, God answers you: 'I have taken someone away from you who is precious to you, so that I can give you the greatest, the most precious Person: Myself. I want to be your One and All. Believe Me and you will experience how Jesus will become your complete Satisfaction and the Joy of your life.'

17

God loves us as a Father. Therefore, He takes care that times of refreshment always follow difficult times. His love has already prepared a table for His children in the presence of their enemies and troubles. After times of tears they should be happy and rejoice. Therefore, in times of suffering let us look forward to the times of happiness which will most definitely follow. Then we will overcome the oppressing power of sadness.

If someone wants to prove his gratitude to us, he might say: 'Tell me what you would like, and I will fulfill your wish.' But who can understand that God says to us men, who hurt Him, rebel against Him and forsake Him: "Ask, and it will be given you"? What tremendous love there is behind this offer! It is the love of a Father's heart who enjoys fulfilling the wishes of His children. He is encouraging us to wish for something. For the Father enjoys giving things. Trust in His love, and you will experience the truth of this verse—if you obey His commandments. *Matthew 7:7*

19

Perhaps at this moment there are things in your life which you would like to wish away—people you have to deal with who make life difficult for you—or other problems and troubles. Listen! All of this wants to challenge you to take advantage of a possibility which you have neglected up until now: Take all your problems and difficulties to prayer! There is no unanswered prayer. Persevere in prayer until the aid comes! And it will come indeed, because God in His love is always ready to help you. He is only waiting for you to come to Him.

20

What is the sign of great love? Always wanting to be near the person you love and share everything with him. God the Father loves us like this. We as sinners and godless men by nature are valued so highly by Him that if we return home to Him as overcomers, He will open the gate to the city of God for us. There the Father wants us to dwell with Him forever. Who can comprehend such grace? Live with this hope. Then all your troubles will fade away in the face of the glory of heaven!

Your heart cries aloud: 'I don't feel like it any more. I've had enough. It's too much; it's too difficult.' God, your Father, speaks to you lovingly: 'I am waiting for people who will trust Me in darkest night and go the way that I lead them to the very end.' Do not desert; do not leave your path, not even inwardly through grumbling or self-pity. The price you have to pay is eternal glory. But thank God, your Father, for loving you and leading you along this way, so that He can give you His glory one day.

22

In the face of the times that will descend upon the earth God, the Father, is waiting for people who will trust Him completely. They are the ones who will be able to experience in times of trouble that He is faithful. For it is written in His Word: "They that put their trust in him shall understand the truth: and such as be faithful in love shall abide with him: for grace and mercy is to his saints, and he hath care for his elect." He will care for them in the most difficult times and give them all His love. *Wisdom of Solomon 3:9*

23

You complain that God lets you wait so long before He helps you. How could that be? God, as a true Father who loves you, leads His child intentionally into a school of waiting. There He wants to give you special gifts: patience, humility, steadfast faith. These are the traits of Jesus. He wants to adorn you with them so that you may be resplendent when you come to His throne. God wants to give you more than just the help that you are expecting—which you will receive in His time—therefore, the long school of waiting and suffering. So thank Him for it.

Your life seems to be a mess. You do not know how to straighten it out. Turn to Someone else who can do it. Think of the One who created a wonderful world out of chaos. Should He not be able to straighten out your small life?

He loves you more than His whole creation. He has created you in His image. You are His child, whom He wants to help and set straight. He sent His Son, because He knew what a mess our lives are in, because we act according to our own will and strength, because we oppose His divine ordination and continually give in to sin. Now He is calling to you: 'Jesus is your Redeemer. He loosens your chains, solves your problems and difficulties and answers your questions. Trust Him completely.'

25

God listens to every cry that comes to Him from a human heart. However most people do not listen to God's answer. Ultimately they do not expect any response to their cries. They perish in their need. They are deaf to everything else. Therefore, God is calling to us: Listen to Me. I want to answer your cry for help. Become quiet. Read in My Word. Then you will hear My voice.

26

God, who is Love, has the fullness of gifts and grace to impart. He does not want to keep anything for Himself. He wants to distribute them to His children. However, He is waiting for us to come with open hands. He wants us to let go of the things that our hands are trying to hold on to. He can only lay His gifts into empty hands. And He is longing to give us these gifts. Are we waiting to receive? Are we emptying our hands and stretching them out towards God?

You ask: 'How should I hear the voice of God?' Above all, believe that God wants to speak to you. Expect Him to. God loves you. That is why He inclines Himself to you and is close to you even when you do not sense anything. Observe where the Spirit of God leads you when you read His Word or other spiritual literature. Consider it prayerfully. Write down how God convicts you, how He shows you His grace and His promises, how He calls you to dedication. Renounce the things you are bound to and say a prayer of faith. Speak with God about everything, as a child would speak with his earthly father or a friend with his friend. He will not only answer, but He will do more than you could ever ask.

28

You say you are too weak and too pitiful. That is why you cannot believe. It is just the other way around. You are still too strong; you expect too much from yourself. Those who have become so small that they think they are nothing, can do nothing else but cling to God's help. And that is faith. Desire to be small, needy and weak like a little child. Then you will be able to believe. Then you will experience help from God your Father.

29

God, the Father, is Love. That is why He takes such great pains to form us, His children, into the image of His love. So, if you should have to live with a difficult person, realize that is the leading of God. Now, as your Father, God is about to develop His image of love in you. Something great will happen to you that has lasting value for time and eternity. Thank Him for working on your soul. Then you will be helped, and the image of God, the image of love, will be formed within you.

God wanted to strengthen our faith by revealing to us who He is. The Apostle John expresses it concisely: "God is love." So whenever you have to suffer deeply or take paths that you do not understand, say and sing again and again: "God is Love; God is Love." If you say this confession or sing it before the visible and also before the invisible world, your trust in the Father will become invincible and you will be comforted in the greatest suffering. *1 John 4:16*

OCTOBER 1

God, the Father, always has a tender, loving word to speak to His child who is in need. He calls to him: "Fear not, you worm of Jacob, I will help you, says the Lord." Or: "My chosen, My beloved, My children." These words show us the love of the Father's heart. Whoever lets himself be taken into this love will be healed of all the needs of his soul. Eat these words like food, and you will really taste how good the Lord is. *Isaiah 41:14*

2

God is a true Father. A good, earthly father pays attention even to the smallest thing which his child does. How much more does our Father in heaven do that! The smallest thing that we do in secret—a small sacrifice, an act of love—God notices it and keeps it in His heart. And one day it will happen as it is written: He will "reward you openly" on the day of the Last Judgment, when He as the great Rewarder will distribute the favours. Should not God's love, which rewards us sinners for the smallest deed and "has put every tear in his bottle", overwhelm us? Consider this love in the darkest hours. Then your trust will know no bounds, just as God's love knows no bounds and limits. *Matthew 6:4. Ps. 56:8*

God's incomprehensible will, which judges and punishes us, can only be recognized as the will of love by those who are His children. Children, who know the heart of the Father, are able to discover the love of the Father in all His leadings and judgments. Our attitude towards God's will shows clearly how we stand: Strangers and servants protest defiantly when the will of God is difficult or incomprehensible for them. Are we children or are we servants?

4

You long to please the Father. You can actually do this. Through His Son God has shown us the way. Jesus went the way of service and obedience. He humbled Himself by letting Himself be baptized in the River Jordan, and the Father said that He was well pleased in Him. Choose this way, and the Father's eyes will rest upon you with pleasure.

5

Your problems are increasing. You do not know how you are going to take care of all of them. The Lord says to you: 'You are not the one who has to solve them. I Myself will take care of them. And no matter how great they are, they cannot be greater than I am. As your Father, I am greater than everything and can take care of every problem. 'Simply believe that.

6

God has hidden a treasure in every cross and in every suffering He gives you. It is up to you to discover it. Count on such priceless treasures, just as a child would expect his father to give him presents. Believe in the love of God! Then you will discover precious treasures in every cross, and suffering will lose its power. You will be refreshed and comforted by God.

You have to go along a difficult path of suffering. You no longer know how you are going to manage it. There is one possibility. With every painstaking step say: 'I praise the blessing, their worth confessing, the paths of pain and darkest night. God's will is goodness and loving-kindness, So good the ways by which He leads.' Then your heart will be comforted, and a new and wonderful life will be born out of the night.

8

If we are called to be the children of God and to know the Father well, we should become sensitive to the suffering of His fatherly heart. It is the heart which bears more sorrow and wounds than any other heart. For to the extent that someone loves, is he capable of suffering. And no one can love as much as God, the Father, because God is Love, Therefore, trust Him in everything; give Him the honour. That will comfort His sorrowful heart.

9

You believe in your Lord Jesus Christ. That makes you a child of God, a beloved one of the Lord. His loving care and help belong especially to His beloved. The Father pays special attention to them. Think of these things whenever you think of the catastrophes which are threatening our times. Cling to the promises of God: "The beloved of the Lord, he dwells in safety by him; he encompasses him all the day long." Yes, He will protect him as only a father could protect his child, his beloved, when he is in need.

Deuteronomy 33:12

You have suffered defeats. You have fought, but without success. God in His love always has a way to help you, and His ways of help are often retroactive. Sing of victory—especially now in the face of defeat when you cannot see any victory. And your defeat will be transformed into victory, for faith can achieve great things even retroactively. It has such great power, because it draws upon the great love of the Father. Faith transforms defeat into victory.

11

Isaiah testifies: "No eye has ever seen a God besides thee, who works for those who wait for him." Yes, the Father works for us, because He is Love. He even works for us when He sends us something that at first makes us think He is against us. But believe that everything the Father does will serve for the best. That applies all ways, including chastisement. It is especially through such discipline that He saves us from sin that brings us so much distress and misfortune, keeping us from being secure and happy in His love even in the midst of all storms and needs.

12

Jesus once said: "I do as the Father has commanded me, so that the world may know that I love the Father. Rise, let us go hence." Jesus put His words into action. In obedience to the Father's command He went to Gethsemane and Calvary. He did this to show the world that He loved the Father. For us as His disciples there is only one way to prove our love for our heavenly Father—with complete determination and fervent love to go the way of the cross which God has designed for us. Jesus is waiting for His disciples to follow Him.   *John 14:31*

Meditate often on the love of God the Father. Then this love will gain room in you, and you will know that you are surrounded by the love of God. Whatever you think of in your heart—whether it be thoughts of love or thoughts of mistrust and bitterness—will gain power over you.

14

Because God is Love, there is only one thought in His heart: He wants to make us happy. He does not want to make us happy for just a short time, but forever. That is why He does not spare us and avoid punishing us with blows of judgment now during this short time on earth. For all eternity He wants to give us the joy of the redeemed. We have a choice: Do we want a short and dull happiness here on earth or do we want everlasting joy in heavenly glory?

15

You say: 'I have put all my energy into praying for these concerns. But God does not answer! It really is all no use.' Do not say that. If you are a child, you will continue to knock and beg. That is the sign of humility. God gives grace to the humble. The Lord listens to humble, childlike prayers.

However, the Lord sometimes answers differently than you think He should. But He will always listen and always take care of your need in one way or another. It may be that He changes your heart and your ways of thinking. Then your needs will no longer depress you. Or your wishes and desires will no longer be so strong, so that if they are not fulfilled, you are no longer tormented. Thus, your heart will be at peace.

'Love Me!' The Lord is asking you to love Him. You are sad, because you cannot sense any love in you. However, love is not revealed in feelings, but in obedience and in faithful endurance during periods of temptation. Simply by your steadfastness you can show God you love Him. Love means always to choose God and His way. Do that, and you will love God and fulfil His command. So He will keep His promise to you. He will love you in return and come and dwell within you.   *John 14:23*

17

Who will be strong and not perish in fear during times of great tribulation? Those who have learned how to say the name, 'Father, dearest Father' lovingly in their hearts. Those who now live in childlike trust in their everyday life, no matter what their needs are, will become strong and experience the help of the Father when they call upon His name in times of great tribulation. Practise living with the Father now and calling upon His name with confidence. This name will prove its power and help even in the deepest night of suffering.

18

In the Old Testament God promises His people: "I will dwell among the people of Israel, and will be their God." And Jesus says to His disciples: "Lo, I am with you always, to the close of the age" to help, to comfort, to admonish. During the day say often: 'Jesus, You are here and You will help me!' Then you will experience that just as in Biblical times God will give you what you need.

Exodus 29:45. Matthew 28:20

Does God's heart seem to be closed to you? There is a way to open it. It is thanksgiving. Thanksgiving is the sign of humble love. The humble are astonished when someone does them even the smallest favour; they do not think they are worthy. The humble respond to the slightest bit of attention, help and kindness with loving thanks and seek to repay the giver. Begin to thank God for all the small things that happen to you, for they always come from His hands. Write them down. This thanks will open God's heart wide and streams of blessing will come down upon you.

20

You have been offended; your heart is wounded. You brood over how your rights will come to light, how you can receive satisfaction. Consider this fact: There is Someone who sees what has been done to you: God, who sees everything. Someone knows what it means to suffer injustice: Jesus. However, the Father brought His rights to light by letting Him arise in splendour as Victor over all His enemies. Therefore join the Psalmist in saying: "For thou hast maintained my just cause; thou hast sat on the throne giving righteous judgment!" Lay your cause into God's hands; let Him maintain your just cause. He will do it, because He is your Father, who loves you and will take care of you. But do what you should do. Do not take revenge; rather pray that bitterness does not gain any room in your heart. "Love your enemies and pray for those who persecute you." Through this you will learn how to love your enemies.

Psalm 9:4. Matthew 5:44

21

You no longer see any solution to your difficulties. However, despondency has never changed things, nor brought anyone to the goal. Therefore, trust that God has a solution for you. Trust has always been able to change things.

If our life runs smoothly without difficulties, that could mean that we have very little contact with God. Thank Him for difficulties. They are meant to bring us into a living relationship with the Father, to draw us to His fatherly heart and to make our spiritual life come alive again. He wants to use them to make us happy children of God. Learn this lesson from periods of need.

23

God our Father is expecting His children to be dedicated to His will in obedience. Our security, our happiness depends upon this dedication of will. For then our will is united with God, then our whole being will become one with Him. If God is leading you along a way which goes against your will and wishes, He is challenging you to surrender your will to Him. He wants to give you the great gift of being one with Him in will and your whole being.

24

God can transform need into abundance, just as Jesus multiplied the bread and fish so that everyone had enough to eat. Up until this very day God multiplies meagre portions —but for whom? The disciples were not allowed to eat the few loaves and fishes, that they had gathered, by themselves. They had to distribute them to the multitudes. In giving them away the loaves and the fish were multiplied and all were filled, including the disciples. So give things away and you will receive. But, first place what you have in the hand of God, as the disciples placed the bread into the hands of Jesus. Then the little bit that you give Him lovingly and trustingly will be increased by His blessing hands so that "the jar of meal shall not be spent." Do this in times of need as well.   *I Kings 17:14*

God, the Father, wants to have His children close to Him. He sends us various troubles and blows of fate in order to bring us home to Him. But we usually do not want these messengers who are sent to bring us home. We get angry and spiteful. And then we wonder why we do not receive the love, gifts and help which we expected from the Father— we wonder why He seems to be far away from us.

In every difficulty caused by situations or by people, let us hear the voice of the love of God calling to us: 'Turn around, come home!' And let us really turn around. The fatherly love of God longs for us. He wants to draw us into fellowship with Him. He wants to make us truly happy in this intimate union with God for which He created us and for which Jesus Christ has redeemed us. So accept the messenger which He sends you.

26

You no longer see a way out of your needs. Count on your Father, who is a creative Lord. In the midst of distress and darkness where there seems to be no way out He is calling forth: "Fiat! Let there be!" What seems to be impossible today will be brought about through such a creative word spoken by God. So ask your Father to say: "Fiat! Let there be!"

27

Who will be so firmly grounded that when the floods of the storm rage across the earth they will not be swept along? They are the people who have built their lives like a house upon a rock, upon the firm foundation of the will of God and His commandments. Whoever does the will of God daily and takes His commandments as the standard for his life will gather building material for a house that will stand firmly. It will not fall even in times of great affliction.

Whoever has difficulty believing in the merciful love of God should consider that God wants to reward us in heaven for even the very smallest things, although He actually does not have to reward us for anything. What would happen to us, if God wanted to weigh according to our deeds! If He put all our sins into one scale and everything we have sown out of love for Him into the other, the scale with the sin would be much heavier. And still He rewards us for the smallest cup of cold water that we have given to one of our brothers. When we are faced by the multitudes of our sins, this will help us to believe that God does not act according to our sins, but according to His great mercy.

29

Want to be poor, incapable and weak. With the strength of God—so the Lord tells us—you can accomplish far greater things than you could relying upon your own human strength no matter how great it might be. Living with Him and drawing upon His strength you will bring forth more fruit and achieve greater things than you could with your own capabilities. So thank Him for wanting to give you His strength in your weakness.

30

God judges us and punishes us, because He is a real Father. That is His love. Through such judgment He saves us from a bit of hell, not only in eternity, but also now. Here on earth we can experience a bit of hell, if we live in bitterness, anger, greed and lust. But God wants to bring us His heavenly joy now in this life. If we let ourselves be cleansed, if we repent of our sins, our life will be changed. Enmity will turn to peace, selfishness to love for others, and a bit of heaven will dawn.

You say: 'I always have trouble believing.' You cannot believe because ultimately you expect everything from yourself and your own capabilities, from people and human resources. But now you have exhausted all these resources. And that is good. Do not seek and expect anything more from yourself or from other people. Now the time has come when God wants to prove His might and help. Perceive them in faith, and circumstances will be transformed.

NOVEMBER 1

When we are depressed, in inner conflict and distress, we should think of the command: 'Rejoice! Practise joy!' Joy has to be practised and God challenges us to practise it. He knows that depression and melancholy make us weak and He wants to make us strong. Strength is the joy of the Lord.

So rejoice in the Lord by beginning to give thanks for the fatherly love of God, who cares for the birds under the sky and much more for you, His child. Thank Him for loving you and forgiving you for the sake of Jesus' sufferings. Then joy will fill your heart. This joy can never be taken from you, because it stems from God, who is eternal. Then you will become stronger and conquer.   *Nehemiah 8:10*

2

There is a question which will test whether we have really become children of God through our Lord Jesus Christ: Do we always think that the will of the Almighty is the will of our loving Father—no matter what the situation is? The will of the Father is always filled with tender and loving care for His children. He never acts like a cold-hearted despot. When children of God are punished by blows of judgment, they are also comforted by this assurance.

Tribulation like never before is threatening to descend upon us. And if I fled to the farthest part of the earth, even there the nuclear powers, which can destroy everything, could reach me. There is only one hiding place; "In the shadow of thy wings I will take refuge, till the storms of destruction pass by." The wings which cover me are the mercy of God. Take refuge there with all those who belong to you. They will surround you lovingly. God is stronger than all other powers. He can command them at His will.

Psalm 57:2

4

We worry and fret about things, but we have no good reason to do so. The troubled and fearful can be lifted out of all their worries. They have the privilege of saying "Father" to God, the Almighty. The job of a father is to take care of his children. Are we taking care that we are really children in our relationship to God? Then He will prove that He is really a Father to us.

5

Blessed are those who are children of God, children of the Father through Jesus Christ in the truest sense of the word. They will be spared the agony that is caused by doubting whether the will of God, when it has to punish severely, is still love. Children are certain that the Father's punishment stems from love. They sense this love, because they can sense how grieved His heart is over their evil deeds and over the necessity to punish. Let yourself be humbled so that you will become as small as a child and every time you are punished, you will rest in the will of the Father. Then the punishments will serve towards your salvation.

When are you strong? When you trust God. But you will be weak when you mistrust Him. So be courageous in faith, and obstacles will fall. Think highly of the power and love of God and you will experience great things from His help and love. Only those who do not rely upon God are forsaken by Him.

7

Did you pray this morning? Perhaps you think: 'I cannot pray. Prayer does not have any sense. God does not hear me! I am too bad.'—You are wrong. He does hear. But it is a matter of dialing the right number, if you want to call someone up. So begin your prayer by dialing the number which will reach the heart of God. Confess to Him how poor and sinful you are, what you have done wrong, where you sinned recently, and what has cast a shadow upon your life. Tell God who you are and what you have done.

But pluck up your courage and make a radical confession to a spiritual counsellor. Guilt must be brought to light and confessed. Then you will receive forgiveness, redemption and release. God, who loves you and cannot bear to see you unhappy, is waiting for you to come to Him. In His arms He embraces all those who confess their sins. Their prayers will be answered, because there is no unforgiven guilt that stands between them and God.

8

Times of suffering and chastisement are times of preparation and that is why they are not endless. Even here on earth times of joy and laughter will follow. The latter are a foretaste. They show us that after this life with its times of preparation there will be eternal rejoicing in His kingdom. Let us live in anticipation of this.

You sense that we are approaching the hour of midnight. It is getting darker and darker on earth. Torches of war and Christian persecution are beginning to blaze. Demonic powers are racing across the earth and are urging people to sin and disregard the law. You are getting scared. But the Lord is speaking to you: 'Do not fear. Just have faith.' By faith the people of God crossed the Red Sea as though they were on dry land. By faith you will also pass through the waves of these times as though you were on dry land. By faith you will experience wonders through Him who is the same yesterday, today and in all eternity.

10

There are no words to express what Jesus has gained for us through His sacrifice on Calvary. We have now become children of God. He has released us from the servitude of legalism so that we may live freely and naturally, trusting in the love of the Father. Whenever someone loves the Father, all legalism and joylessness must yield.

Let the Father love you, and love Him in return. Then you will be happy as a child of God, and you will be led by His Spirit in all matters. Through such natural, carefree and child-like joy you will entice others to come home to the Father. Nothing has such convincing power over others as true childlikeness.

11

Why does the heavenly Father say so much about reward? Reward is the good news which love brings. Love always has to give rewards, even when there is not much to reward. God Himself does this with such overflowing goodness. And we as children of the Father should follow His example of love, as Jesus challenges us when He says: "You, therefore, must be perfect, as your heavenly Father is perfect."

Matthew 5:48

The love of God is down to earth like the love of a true Father. It pursues our weaknesses relentlessly. It can be hard when our stony heart needs a hard hammer. It can be hard, because it is true love that will not rest until the beloved child has become beautiful. See the great love of the Father behind His blows. That will make His punishments seem mild. Do not resist when His hand wants to smash the stone of your heart through His instruments, your difficult fellow men. You make His work difficult and you make it last longer when you resist it. It will be your own harm and disadvantage. Say Yes to His chastisement which you need in order to reach the goal, and you will help His love bring you there more quickly.

13

Perhaps you have asked the Father for something so earnestly and tenderly. And yet He has not answered your prayer. Could the obstacle be on your side? It cannot be the Father's fault. He enjoys giving us things. However, He will only answer our prayers, if we behave like His children, keep His commandments and do what pleases Him. If we are obedient, trusting children, He will prove Himself as a Father in all things.

14

When the threatening destruction is about to capture all your thoughts, the Lord calls to you: 'Do not look at the destruction, but look at your Lord who will come again and establish His kingdom. He is nigh and will take you with Him.' God does not say: 'I will strengthen those who look at the tribulation and the coming wars.' No, His Word teaches us to do the opposite: "I will look to the Lord, my God will hear me." So look to God, the Father, who loves you and promises that He will be with you and help you in your affliction. *Micah 7:7*

You are sitting in front of a mountain of worries. However the Lord says to you: 'It is your own fault that your needs are about to crush you.' No one has to remain in misery. Only those who do not bring their needs and worries to Him and count on His help will remain in need. You will only receive the help which you trust the Father to give.

16

The parable of the Prodigal Son tells us something. There is Someone who is interested in you, Someone to whom you are dear and precious, Someone who is looking to see whether you will turn to Him. He is waiting for your voice. He is waiting for you to place your hand in His fatherly hand. He wants to help you. Will you come?

17

We are not in the hands of the warfaring powers. We are in the hands of God the Father who alone can make wars cease. It is within our means to turn the hand of God, if it is stretched out for judgment, through prayer, through contrition and repentance. But who takes advantage of this offer? God, the Father, is waiting for people to pray and move His heart and hands so that He can once more grant us and our people a period of grace.

18

You are tempted. It is difficult for you to believe in God's love. It was the Prodigal Son who returned home that recognized the heart of the Father and could believe in His abundant love. His tears of repentance and his confession of sin opened his eyes to see who the Father is—pure Love. That is also the way for you to recognize the Father in His love. On the way of contrition your temptation will yield.

Worrying shows that we think we are important. We think that everything depends upon us alone. We think that we have to take things into our own hands and to settle them by ourselves. However, those who have their anchor in the Father as true children, do not count upon their own ways and means, but upon the Father's power. When we count on Him, our worries will disappear.

20

God resists the high and mighty. They stand in the way of God's greatness and doings with their own importance. Therefore, become a child. God is gracious to the small and lowly. He comes to them. He loves the poor and the weak. The beloved of God sit in His lap. May this assurance suffice if you belong to the small, weak and lowly.

21

You think that when a nuclear war begins there will be no way out. But love always knows a way out as long as its power to help is sufficient. God, the Father, loves us as no person could, and has power even when man no longer has any. Therefore, He always has a way out of your needs. So look for the way out; it will certainly come.

22

You say that God is against you. You cannot do anything right, You have no success. But it is exactly now that God intends to do something great with you. He wants to put your hip out of joint as He did to Jacob, so that as a pardoned person you may go forth to the rising sun, to a new and brilliant morning.

Do not count on your own strength or your own abilities. They are really not sufficient. Count on God. His ability and His strength will always be sufficient for you. In His love and omnipotence He has as much strength and help prepared for you as you need.

24

God leads you into hopeless situations to teach you how to believe. For if you can see how He is going to help you, you do not have to believe. Only when there is nothing to be seen can you believe. Therefore, believe! Believe again and again! Endure in faith and the hour will come when you can see what you have believed. "Wait for the Lord, and he will help you."
Proverbs 20:22

25

The fatherly heart of God rejoices over a child who says to Him in faith, before he sees the answer to his prayers: 'I know that You will help me. I thank You that I can count on Your help'—say this, and you can be certain that the Father will not disappoint such trust.

26

God gives you burdens in your personal life and in your ministry. So believe that He also takes over the responsibility to give you what you need to deal with these burdens. He is not a hard Master, demanding you to do something without giving you His help. He knows exactly what you need for this situation and will give it to you. But those who say in their hearts: 'You are a hard Master' will not receive a new source of strength. They will close off the help of God through their own unbelief, their grumbling and their defiant protests.

Are you discontented? That cannot be according to the will of God. For God, who loves His creatures and children, wants to make them happy and contented. He is showing you a way which will certainly lead to satisfaction. He is asking you first: 'Where does your dissatisfaction come from?' You know the proverb: "The more you have, the more you want." The more you want to have for yourself, the more dissatisfied you will be. That is a law. But the more you give to God in the way of time, energy, love, esteem and rights, the more satisfied you will be.

That is the way to which Jesus has called us. "He who finds his life will lose it, and he who loses his life for my sake will find it." When you begin to give up things instead of trying to claim your rights and to demand things from God and man, you will experience how God's wonderful plans for your life are being fulfilled. Act accordingly. Then your dissatisfaction will yield, and peace and joy will fill your heart. *Matthew 10:39*

28

It is the hand of the kindest Father which leads us. Everything that we have comes from Him. Whoever has learned to accept everything from the hand of the Father remains quiet through all difficulties and troubles. He knows that the Father's kind hand leads him lovingly upon difficult ways and that His strong arm will sustain him.

29

God is the Father of the small and lowly. Through them He performs His greatest works. Desire to be small, and He will use you for great things.

NOVEMBER

The fact that God is the Father of love means that His will is always kindness. His will comes from a heart full of love. Worship and praise His will as the will of kindness. Worship His will even if He leads you along difficult and incomprehensible ways and you experience bitter disappointment. In worship and praise that which is bitter will become milder, it will even become sweet.

DECEMBER

1

God is laying a heavy cross upon you. You would like to shake off this oppressive burden. Know that only the proud want to do this. They think they do not need this. But the humble know how much they need punishments and how good and wholesome the cross is for them. You can choose: Your cross can oppress you, if you do not want to bend down beneath it. But it can also become light and bring you joy if you praise the blessing that your cross will bring you. It is for the sake of your eternal joy that the Lord gave it to you.

2

Your life is like a ship. It is tossed about by a storm. You are afraid. You call to God. But the storm grows stronger. The waves are threatening to swallow you up. You cry: 'Where is my God? Has He not heard my prayer?' He has heard it. But often it is His will to let the storm reach its climax. He is doing it on purpose—out of love. He wants to receive as much faith as possible from you, in order to be able to hand you the crown of faith one day. According to your faith, He wants to let His miracles take place today. He wants to magnify His holy name.

So when the storm shakes you, be brave and praise Him: Now God is at work. Now great things will happen to me. His name will be glorified. I will endure and trust Him.

Strangers and servants do not have access to the treasures in the Father's house—only children do. But, you can only become a child through faith in your Redeemer, Jesus Christ. The cross is the gate leading to the Father's house. Bring your sins to the cross, by being sorry for them and confessing them before God and man. Then the gate will open and the riches of the Father's house will belong to you.

4

You complain that your Christian life has so little power and authority, so little effect upon others. It must be *your* fault. For God in His great love is only interested in bringing us blessing and power. That is why He sent His beloved Son. He redeemed us to bear fruit and bring blessings to others. He shows you the way.

Begin to offer sacrifices for God and His kingdom, sacrifices which cost you something. If you offer up your time and energy, trust Him to give you more time and to renew your strength. If you sacrifice money and possessions for Him and His kingdom, trust Him to give you all you need in a different way. Then you will experience the love of God as never before, and you will become a bearer of blessing for others.

5

You count upon God's help as far as you can reasonably understand it. But trust God that He has ways to help you that far surpass your understanding. Count on His omnipotence and He will do wonders and great deeds that are beyond human understanding. Then you will be counting on the right thing.

Fear of the coming times is depressing you. The Lord says to you: 'Have I not told you that I will be with you always? Thus the days of affliction will be no exception. On the contrary I will be closer to you than ever before. If the affliction is seven times greater than usual, My help will also be seven times greater. During the most difficult days I will come with even greater hosts of angels to help you.' You can rely upon this. God's presence will be closer and His help stronger than ever before.

7

Each day brings something different. This day will bring you certain joys and sorrows. The next day will bring you different ones. But nothing that happens to you is merely a matter of coincidence. Not even the smallest event, not even the smallest incident in your life. Indeed, "does evil befall a city, unless the Lord has done it?" He has forgotten nothing in the plan for your life, for your day. Everything is perfect.

Therefore, see the Father's actions in everything that happens to you. Whatever comes from Him has to be filled with blessing and serve for the best. Whoever accepts everything that God places in his day with love and thanksgiving will be richly blessed by the love of God—even through things that are hard for him. *Amos 3:6*

8

When suffering is about to get you down, remember that it does not stem from a blind power of fate, but comes from the Father's hand. Begin to praise God, the Father, for giving you suffering that will bring glory. Suffering is meant to transform us into the image of God and to help us reap a great harvest. So say to the Father: 'I want to suffer. It will help prepare me for eternal glory.' Then blessing and comfort will immediately flow into your heart.

The greatest present God the Father wants to give us is love. He knows that love makes us happy. That is why He has brought it to us through Jesus Christ. Whoever can love will win the hearts of men, because people cannot resist love forever.

Whoever has love has peace in his heart, even when people are hostile towards him and cause external strife. Love can endure all, be patient and even do good to his enemy. Crucify your self-love daily, so that there will be room for the love of God through Jesus Christ in you—and you will have everything.

10

Powers and dominions are raging upon this earth. It has become dark. But there is Someone who is watching over us. It is the Father. And a loving heart, the heart of the Father, speaks to us: "I will be with him in trouble." That is enough. *Psalm 91:15*

11

Many people do not know what a childlike prayer is, even though they call God their Father through personal faith in Jesus Christ. They neglect to turn from their ways of self-importance and independence, from their rebellion against punishment, from their yearning for recognition and power. With such an attitude how could they really be children of the Father? Only children can pray and receive God's gifts. God only gives grace to the humble. The prayers of the little ones rise through the clouds. So commit yourself to being a true child, to being made small and humble. Then your prayer will have power.

You are filled with fear. God could demand a sacrifice from you. He could take something from you that is precious to you. This fear is tearing you to pieces. You cannot be happy. But, trust God! How could He whose heart is goodness and love demand something from you that would ultimately only make you unhappy? That is impossible. Therefore, sacrifice something to God voluntarily in complete trust. When you give Him things in this manner, you will become strong and happy. God does not take anything without giving something in return. He will reward you richly.

13

To love God means to surrender ourselves to Him completely with our whole being and life, with all our energy, with all our thoughts. Because Jesus had such love, He also had an urgent longing to surrender His life. This same yearning is in all true disciples of Jesus, who love God. Such disciples are the true children of God; God gives them power and authority in His kingdom. They will experience that just as the sacrifice of the sons of the land save the fatherland, so the commitment of the sons of God saves His Church.

14

Before our eyes the Son of God is hanging on the cross. God delivered up His dearest Son to such a dreadful death. The cross tells us how much God the Father loves us. It gives us the guarantee that all His difficult ways of chastisement are only blows of love, which seek to prepare us for glory. Therefore, look at the cross on Calvary, and you will gain a glimpse into the heart of God the Father. His love will overwhelm you and you will stop doubting His love.

A father who loves his child does not want him to be bad or unpleasant. But there is no human father who loves his child as much as the heavenly Father loves us. He makes every effort to make our souls beautiful. Shouldn't we thank Him for His work?

Therefore, when He leads us along paths of suffering, let us renounce all self-pity. Our sorrow, which we have usually earned through our sins, is not worth the tears—but only God's sorrow and work for our sake. Let us begin to thank Him for taking such great pains to bring us up properly, to make us beautiful and happy for all eternity. Then our cross will begin to shine.

16

You feel alone and forsaken. You are afraid. You cannot cope with your present needs nor with the thought of the horrible things to come. But remember, you have become a child of the Father through Jesus Christ. And there is one thing a father cannot do: leave his child alone when he is in need. Nowhere is there such a father, if he is a true father. And even if there were such a father on earth—your Father in heaven could never forsake or ignore you.

17

Jesus calls to us: "Unless you turn and become like children, you will never enter the kingdom of heaven." Nor will you ever attain the treasures of heaven through your requests. So let us turn from our self-importance, our self-security, our self-righteousness and all protests against the will of God and His chastisements. Then our prayers will attain much. Then as children we will attain the treasures of the kingdom of heaven and the gifts of the Father.

Matthew 18:3

Believe! "Do not throw away your confidence!" Believe that God loves you. Believe that He has a way for you, that He has prepared help for you. He will do everything right, because He is a Father. Yes, "believe in him, and he will help thee." Everything depends upon faith. Place your faith in God, who has proved His love for you by delivering up His Son to redeem men from the depths of hell. Should not this Lord, your loving Father, also rescue you from your far smaller problems, even though they may seem like hell to you? Trust Him in your daily life and in the time of catastrophe.   *Hebrews 10:35 Ecclesiasticus 2:6*

19

Do you have great expectations? Great hopes? That is the way Christians are! Expect a present from God. Expect something good, expect help from the Father especially after days of suffering. Be a child, and open your heart and hands wide so that He can give you His gifts. With such expectations and hopes you will not be disappointed.

20

Your difficulties seem to be so great that you do not know how you can deal with them. They are depressing you. But then there must be something wrong. God never gives us more than we can bear. You have lost the correct proportions. Compared to the greatness of God your needs are very small—like a grain of sand compared to a giant mountain. No matter how great your temptations, your problems and your difficulties are, they can never be greater than God in His power and love. Look towards His power and love, which are so much greater than your needs, and count on them. Then your difficulties will become small.

Whoever has lived apart from God and has never been interested in doing His will cannot suddenly say one day: 'From now on I want to turn to the Father. Then everything will be all right.' Such good intentions do not lead anywhere. If I want to begin a new way of dependence upon the Father, I must confess with my whole heart: 'My Father, I have sinned.' Then through the blood of His Son I will be granted forgiveness, and the sin of my life up until now will be wiped out. Then I will be cleansed through the blood of Jesus Christ so that I will no longer live for myself, but for God in blissful dependence, in fellowship with Him. Then everything in my life will become new.

22

God's final plan for your life can never be suffering, distress, worries. No, just the opposite: release, help, comfort, joy. Say these words over and over again in your heart. Say: 'I thank You, God, that Your help is waiting just outside the door.' Then your worries will yield, and you will experience the help of God.

23

You are despondent, because you have exhausted all your energy, talents, contacts and possibilities that gave you courage and self-confidence. That is foolish. Now you can get help from Someone else. There is no end to His help. His energy is inexhaustible. He always knows how to help you and is always prepared to do so.

It is God, Your Father, a Father of love. Turn to Him in prayer. As a Father He will listen to your prayers. He will consider them in His heart and send you help. In His wisdom He will decide what kind of help to send you. In His love He will determine the timing. But he will always help, so that you have to confess afterwards: His Word is yea and amen: "Every one who asks receives." *Matthew 7:8*

Everything seems to be so hopeless. You can only see obstacles, difficulties, impossibilities. Use the bulldozer which can break through all walls of obstacles: the prayer of faith. It is strong. It can accomplish everything, because the One whom you ask can do everything and wants to use His power for you and your difficulties. If you believe that, you will experience it. Wouldn't a father who sees his child in need do everything he can to help him?

25

Be of good cheer. The Father in heaven has sent the One of whom it is written: "I have overcome the world." He has overcome your world, your environment, which brings you so many troubles and difficulties. There is Someone who has come to earth to deal with it—Jesus Christ. God, the Father, has sent Him for you so that He could deal with the problems of your small world. Bring them to Him, and He will act so that you will be astonished at how He was able to solve everything.   *John 16:33*

26

Rejoice every day, like a child looking forward to Christmas! The heavenly Father has surprises of love prepared for you. His greatest gift—that His Son became our Brother—has put the seal on this. As a true, loving Father, He has planned only good things for this day and for your whole life. Full of expectation, begin to look for these things all the time. Then you will find them. You will be thankful and happy and always richly endowed with the love of God.

A servant has to take care that he receives his due from his master—but not a child. A child is obviously entitled to everything that is in his father's house. In all his dilemmas of body and soul he can come to the father. He shares everything that the father possesses. A child lacks nothing if his father is rich.

But who is as rich as our Father in heaven, who makes us sinners His children through His Son Jesus Christ? If we only take care that we become true children of God in love, trust, dependence and obedience, we will be able to share in the riches of God and we will never lack anything.

28

It is written in the Word of God: "... to do good in the end." This was the promise of the desert wanderings of the children of Israel. And it is the outcome of every spiritual desert wandering in our life. Keep your eyes on this and you will experience this truth.   *Deuteronomy 8:16*

29

As a loving Father, God would like to hold a conversation with you, His child. He is waiting for you to come to Him in prayer, to pour out your heart to Him. He is waiting for you to hear what He has to say to you through His Word. What a loss, if you do not take advantage of this opportunity faithfully! Only these quiet times apart with God, these conversations of love, can make you strong to overcome your daily problems. Keep them faithfully—fellowship with God will make you invincible.

God has granted each of us a definite time to live upon this earth. It is short—at most several decades. The love of God which wants to reward you one day gives you opportunities every day to sow many seeds. Which are the hours that will have brought a rich harvest? Hours which you have dedicated to Him. So as proof of your love, give Him more time. He is waiting for it and He will reward you for it—both here and in eternity.

Every merchant knows that he has to keep his books balanced. Have you ever considered balancing the books of your life—for instance, your relationship to God and your fellow man over the past year? One day you will have to balance your books. But then it can be too late, because judgment will follow and the wrath of God will strike you. However, the love of God has not destined us for wrath, but for salvation.

Today you still have a chance to balance the books of your life. Today you can turn from your evil ways. You can confess before God and man what was not right and set it straight as far as you are able. You can commit yourself to suffer for your sins. You can call upon Jesus to cover the deficits of your life. What an opportunity God is giving you! His love cannot bear to see you get lost. Do not postpone this settlement of accounts! Tomorrow may be too late!

I Thessalonians 5:9